"This book is a must-read for anyone looking to super-charge their healing! Elle sees the importance of how we think, feel, and choose, and how this impacts how we function in our day-to-day lives. *How We Heal* is a natural outpouring of her passion for helping others find true and lasting healing through the power of the mind."

—Dr. Caroline Leaf, neuroscientist, bestselling author, and award-winning podcast host

"This beautiful book is the physical manifestation of Elle's work—the power of healing through community. The book takes us on the journey of witnessing powerful and vulnerable stories while inviting us to look at our own healing. You'll finish this book feeling like you just left an intimate event with some of the most wonderful voices in wellness and beyond."

—Yasmine Cheyenne, self-healing educator, author, and mental wellness advocate

We Heal

Uncover Your Power and Set Yourself Free

ALEXANDRA ELLE

Illustrations by Laxmi Hussein

CHRONICLE BOOKS

SAN FRANCISCO

Text copyright © 2022 by Alexandra Elle.

Illustrations copyright © 2022 by Laxmi Hussein.

Library of Congress Cataloging-in-Publication Data available.

ISBN 978-1-7972-1626-3

Manufactured in China.

Design by Vanessa Dina.

Editorial direction by Rachel Hiles and Sarah Billingsley.

Typesetting by Howie Severson.

10 9 8 7 6 5 4 3 2 1

Chronicle books and gifts are available at special quantity discounts to corporations, professional associations, literacy programs, and other organizations. For details and discount information, please contact our premiums department at corporatesales@chroniclebooks.com or at 1-800-759-0190.

Chronicle Books LLC
680 Second Street
San Francisco, California 94107
www.chroniclebooks.com

For my readers

When we heal ourselves, we heal our lineage.
Healing is an act of community care.

For my daughters

I love you beyond words. You are the reason I heal.

3

Reclaiming Your Power 98

4

Healing Your Heart 148

For years I have been teaching folks from all walks of life how to use writing as a way to heal. I've led self-care workshops throughout the world, and I've helped thousands of people on their healing journeys. And yet this book almost didn't happen. My self-doubt and imposter syndrome were intense. I found myself stuck in a negative thought spiral, asking myself questions like, *Who do you think you are? What makes you think you're qualified to write this? You're no therapist, no doctor, no scholar with a research background. Your experience is not enough.*

With that negative self-talk in tow, I would go to my computer and try my hand at writing a book about healing and self-discovery and self-trust. Every time I sat down to write, my eyes would burn. My heart would beat fast, and my palms would sweat. Anxiety would win time and time again. Most days, walking away felt safer than trying. As I walked away, my self-doubt would say, *See? You're a quitter. That's why this isn't for you. You're not really made for this work.* Wow—intense, right? The stories we tell ourselves can make or break us.

As I started to peel back the layers of why I was trying to talk myself out of writing this book, I began to realize I was concerned about the wrong thing: I was too concerned that my experience isn't enough when it absolutely is. And while I may not have a degree in psychology or a full-time research job, I have real life lived under my belt. I've been hurt, and I have healed—that counts for something. I realized my role is to help people show up authentically in their healing in ways that leave them better than they were before reading this book.

I'm sharing this story because I know for a fact that we all have these moments of doubting who we are, or even forgetting who we are and how far we have come. Sometimes we are our harshest critic. Each of us, at one point in time, has made up stories in our head about who we aren't instead of focusing on the good of who we are. Maybe you're reading this and thinking, *Someone has actually told me those negative things about myself and my capabilities, and I believed them.* No matter where your small self-view comes from, you must remember that in healing and releasing untrue stories and outside projections, shrinking and walking away won't serve you. Healing requires us to get in touch with our true selves—and that, my friends, requires us to show up and be big.

I've been working on my inner critic in therapy for the past couple of years, and healing the part of my mind that tells me I am not good enough is a work in progress. I know I'm not alone there. I've had the honor of facilitating thousands of people on their writing-to-heal journeys. The expansive way that people showed up on the pages of their journals blew my mind each and every time. I saw that, through writing, people could take an honest look at their pain in a way that they never could before. Everyone says the same thing: "I want to find myself, heal my heart, and let go of the things that are getting in the way of that." But so often, people choose not to look at their emotional wounds, traumas, and shortcomings because they don't know how to heal themselves after uncovering the mess.

I get that. I turned away from my pain for years. Turning away led to a lot of destructive behaviors like self-harm, anxiety, depression, and having a child at eighteen because I was looking for love, comfort, and attention in all the wrong places. Healing what tears us open is challenging, but possible, work. Humans are complicated and flawed. I'd like us to normalize that and be open to greeting our fear and imperfections right where they are.

My own healing journey has been rooted in writing to heal—the practice of using writing to unpack my baggage, process my deepest emotions, and create a new narrative for my life. In my personal practice, writing shapes me, and it continues to be my permission to show up flawed and unsure while also holding space for gratitude, potential, and the recognition of how far I've come.

Writing reminds me that I don't need to have my stuff together to start my healing. Instead, it's a reminder to show up as I am with curiosity in hand, ready to take on whatever is in front of me on the page. It is a tool that reminds me that even in doubt, the work I need to do will meet me wherever I am. As I heal, I come to the page raw and honest and remember that I am not a victim of my thoughts. When I thought I couldn't get myself together enough to write this book, the pages of my journal allowed me to uncover not just my *why*, but also my *why not*. Clarity will always find us if we are curious and honest enough. But it won't be without struggle. Healing is slow and sacred work that we will all grapple with in our lifetimes.

The more I explore my own healing, and the longer I teach writing-to-heal courses, the more I've discovered that trauma does not have to be our resting place. We can feel, address, and notice our pain without lying down in it and staying there. To me, that is what it means to walk through, or alongside, our healing, getting back up again whenever we stumble or fall. I used to think that was such a drag—not arriving at a destination of being healed— but the more I got to know myself and my pain points, the more I realized that what is necessary is choosing not to stay in the pit of my pain, looking at it for what it is, and using the tools I share here. There is no end point to healing.

Healing in the wellness community is often talked about as an end goal. The messaging suggests that if we can just heal and get over it (whatever "it" is), all will be well and good. But healing does not mean that you won't experience more suffering or tenderness around the original thing that hurt you. Healing is a forever thing, or like

I say to my clients and students, a constant reminder to love and care for ourselves—an invitation to nurture ourselves just like we do everyone else.

We heal to make space, to redefine ourselves and our narratives. To expand and become better. To forgive, create new possibilities, and move forward. To build community and create bonds. We heal to release shame, manifest self-love, create autonomy, and begin again. We heal to redefine ourselves, face our fears, and develop self-trust. We heal to mend relationships and deepen connections with those around us. We heal to get free.

Healing creates a healthy sense of togetherness in a way that misery and brokenness cannot. I know this to be true because I spent years of my life trauma-bonding with people, and there was nothing healthy about that for them or me. I was codependent and trapped in emotional confusion. Sometimes we heal to prove a point—there is often healing in the proving, changing, and having outsiders bear witness. There may be people in your life not ready to do their own healing work yet, but when they watch you change, break cycles, and start healing, it is almost like a permission slip of what's possible for their own lives.

There were many people in my life who had not done their own healing, and they told me I'd be nothing but a broken teen mom with no life skills. Not only did I refuse to believe that, but I also worked hard to not be what people were hoping I'd be. I will not let outside projections break me.

You may be the only one doing things differently in your family, or you may be the only one deciding to get emotionally free in your friend group. I know this can feel isolating, but do not ignore your healing because you're waiting for your loved ones to get on board. Take action, set boundaries, and do the work because you're the leader of your life and they're the leaders of theirs. Remember, you can love people deeply and still choose not to stay stuck in unhealthy patterns with them. Your self-healing can lead the way for onlookers. It is an open invitation for others to explore what healing can look like in their own lives.

Healing is transformational and cyclical, whether you have a broken arm or a broken heart. Whatever is hurting, breaking, or crumbling must be tended to. Ignoring does not mend us—it causes rapid disintegration of our mind, body, and spirit. If we don't face what is hurting or aching, it will continue to break us down.

I discovered that healing myself was an active choice of learning from my mistakes and remembering my worth. It takes effort. It requires consistently finding the sweet spot of mending for the moment. That's why I say this is a forever thing, a forever love, a marriage of sorts. Trusting that healing was an active choice that can be hard as hell gave me inner peace on the days that hurt the most. When I stopped chasing the idea that I would be forever healed after I healed the first time, the disappointment of not having a whimsical experience vanished. Remembering that I am not broken, that I need to tend to the same thing that I thought I healed from already, offered me a sense of grace.

In this book, I invite you to join me on a healing journey, a journey of reconnecting with yourself and welcoming the joy that shows up at your door. My hope is that this book provides you with the resources to create your own self-healing practice. This is an invitation to find what works and feels good for you. And even though healing can look and feel vastly different to each and every one of us, we all have something in common—the desire to live a life that is fulfilling and liberating, even when the going gets tough.

In the following pages, I will guide you through a four-step healing process. In step 1, we will tend to self-doubt and make room for new beginnings so that we are prepared to walk the path ahead. In step 2, we will work on learning how to befriend our fear so that it no longer controls us. Step 3 offers lessons in reclaiming your power and rewriting your story with intention. And step 4 focuses on leaning in to what feels good so that we can live with gratitude and joy.

This four-step process is the same framework that I've relied on in my own healing journey, and it's a process that has helped thousands of my workshop participants heal their hearts. Though healing is never linear, my hope is that following these steps will provide you with a foundation for healing—building blocks that you can return to again and again.

Throughout each step you'll find writing exercises for you to follow in your journal. Journaling is central to the work we'll be doing together. Maybe you're coming to this book thinking "I'm not a writer" or "I've never been good at journaling." Leave those thoughts behind. Writing to heal is for everyone. Let your journal be your confidant, your companion, and your mirror. A safe place to fall apart and come back together. When we write to heal, we show up for ourselves with no pretense or judgment, and we make space to connect to the deepest, most sacred parts of ourselves.

In addition to the writing exercises, you'll also find conversation prompts, meditations, and breathwork practices. Together, these elements form the backbone of this journey to heal. We write to unpack our baggage, make sense of our pain, and manifest new narratives. We connect with loved ones to build community and find support. We meditate and breathe to release tension in our bodies and make room for healing and joy in our spirit.

Sprinkled throughout the book are essays and interviews from a range of incredible women—writers, athletes, therapists, artists, and more—who have done deep healing work. It is my hope that their stories will offer you hope and inspiration on your own path.

As you work your way through this book, remember that there is always more work to be done. Healing is an act of lineage restoration—facing and repairing the traumas that have been passed down through generations—and that takes time. Even if you are the only one in your family doing the work to heal, do not be discouraged. You are capable of leading the way and setting the tone. This may feel like a lot to carry, but remember, you can always unpack your baggage and leave some things behind. Take some of those old feelings and habits out of your emotional suitcase. If it's not serving you, let it go. Not everyone will understand your commitment to yourself, your well-being, and your healing work. Don't worry about not being understood. Remember why you are healing and keep the promise to yourself to keep going.

And when healing feels complex, complicated, or too much, I invite you to rest. Take a break and come back to what you're attempting to push through, work on, and piece together. Healing isn't about getting it done as fast as you can—it's about pacing yourself, paying attention, and prioritizing your needs. Tending to your healing is an act of self-nurturance that no one else can give you and no one else can do for you. You are capable, even if that means you need to step away for a while to recalibrate.

On our journey together, we'll look at our flaws so that we can face them and heal our emotional wounds in healthy and supportive ways. We will also look at our small moments of joy, healing, and gratitude. Self-celebration is a part of this work too. We will take breaks from the deep healing work on the page and look at our lives through the lens of joy and learn how to identify what makes us feel seen, safe, and supported.

Maya Angelou said, "Nothing will work unless you do." Keep this phrase close. If you want your healing to bring you clarity, you must show up and tend to it—even the messy and gritty. Yes to rest, and also, yes to revisiting. Healing will come in waves, so pay attention to yourself, your body, and your feelings as you work your way through the good and the bad. When we heal ourselves, we start healing our lineage, our communities, and ourselves. That, my friends, is a radical *and* necessary act.

Ten Reasons Why I Heal

In your journal, title the top of your page "Why I Heal." List ten things that come to mind. You can do this all in one sitting or come back to it as things pop into your head. I've given you some prompts below to get your mind working.

I am healing because I want . . .

I am healing because I need . . .

I am healing because I deserve . . .

I am healing because I feel . . .

I am healing because I see . . .

I am healing because I love . . .

I am healing because my . . .

I am healing because I am . . .

I am healing because I can . . .

I am healing because I choose . . .

Journaling

Once your list is complete, pick your top three reasons and write each one on its own sticky note. Place each sticky note somewhere in your living space—kitchen, bathroom mirror, bedside table. You can also take a photo of one and set it as your phone's background. Seeing is not only believing but also remembering. If you need a nudge to get you started, take a look at my completed list.

I am healing because I want **emotional freedom.**

I am healing because I need **clarity.**

I am healing because I deserve **to feel at peace.**

I am healing because I feel **open and ready.**

I am healing because I see **the possibilities of growth.**

I am healing because I love **looking back at how far I've come.**

I am healing because my **children are watching.**

I am healing because I am **committed to breaking unhealthy cycles.**

I am healing because I can **create peace in my life and mind.**

I am healing because I choose **to trust the process and journey ahead.**

1

Starting from Scratch

Healing is a never-ending journey. Even when I think I've moved past something, life throws a curveball my way that takes me right back to a place of self-doubt and negative self-talk. This lesson came up for me recently, during a trip with my dear friend Erika.

Erika and I sat around a wooden table in the quaint house we had rented. We'd been talking about our lives and the many transitions happening for us in motherhood, partnership, and work. She was separated from her husband. I was struggling with being home every single day during the pandemic. Over dinner and a glass of wine, we talked about it all: the good, the bad, the changes, and the struggles. I remember thinking there was something healing about the nonjudgmental safety net of sisterhood. It felt so nice to have uninterrupted girl time.

As the conversation progressed from our current lives to our childhoods, it felt right to start baking the peach cobbler I'd been making for a month straight. I had been raving to Erika about this dessert all day—both of us were excited to dig in.

I hadn't always been interested in cooking. As a kid, the kitchen wasn't a fun place for me. Messes weren't encouraged and I was more in the way than anything else. I would watch my mom bake and cook from afar. For many years, cooking felt more like a forbidden activity than a liberating and sacred practice. Then, when I was in my early twenties, a close friend taught me how to stop overthinking it and instead taste and feel my way around the kitchen. Looking back, that was one of my first adult lessons on self-trust: to not know what I was doing and try anyway. Now, as an adult who loves to bake, especially alongside my children, I've found a lot of healing in starting from scratch, in making messes, with flour on clothes and sugar sweetening the countertops, and in licking the spoon of batter or frosting. Beginning again, each time, to create something that makes smiles big and bellies full—something that nurtures the body and soul.

That is what I looking forward to sharing with Erika, the nourishing experience of coming together over a shared dish made from scratch. When the timer went off for the cobbler, we rushed to the oven, happy and ready to try the dessert. It looked delicious. It was the perfect hue of golden brown, and the sugar had caramelized beautifully. We both could see the butter bubbling like mini eruptions under the crust. I was so excited about how good it looked, I took a photo and sent an enthusiastic text to my mom and grandmother to display my homemade creation.

In response, my mom wrote back, "Your cooking is improving . . ."

"My cooking is improving?" I replied. "I've been cooking and baking for years. I have a whole family to cook for—this isn't a new thing."

The conversation went silent after that.

My blood was boiling, and I was so frustrated with myself for sending them that message. At that moment, I thought, *Of course my mom can never just say, "Alex, that's nice!" or "Great job! How did it taste?" Even a simple "Yum!" would suffice. It always had to be something that would leave me questioning myself.* I looked up from my phone with tears in my eyes, feeling both hurt and foolish for being hurt. Erika asked me what was wrong, and I started sobbing. She wrapped me in a hug. "It's okay, babe," she said in her warm, loving voice. "We all have triggers that we're still working through."

When I got myself together we talked about it. I explained the emotions I had around feeling discredited or not good enough every time I did something, big or small. And even though I'd done so much work to heal and process things, like the relationship with my mother, certain interactions—even a short text message—still sent me spiraling backward.

I told Erika how painful it is to feel like the only mindful one in my family and how challenging and lonely it is to be the matriarch of healing for my lineage. I was frustrated with myself that I hadn't yet gotten to a point of accepting that certain things will always be what they are. Starting from scratch time and time again, just like the baking I love to do, was frustrating rather than rewarding.

The lesson that emerged from this tender moment was that I could either make peace with the reality of my circumstances or continue putting myself in situations where I expect different results, yet know that I won't get them. This doesn't make me or my mother good or bad; it just means that certain things may not change—and that we are different. I was the one with the issue. My mother wasn't suffering like I was. She had no clue that that exchange ruined my night and made me feel invalidated and hurt. I was still healing from childhood wounds that needed my attention. Erika held space for me and listened with a caring ear. She reminded me that our parents do the best they can with what they have, and sometimes their best isn't supportive of our healing in the way that we want or need.

I've grown to know starting from scratch so well that, like baking, it feels restorative now, rather than draining. Nurturing ourselves and our relationships takes dedication, clear communication, and an open heart. When we release control and address our needs and wants, clarity becomes more accessible, even when we're let down, disappointed, or sad. Healing, grief, and pain points all come in waves. Having to start over again in your process doesn't make you weak, undeserving, or unchanged—it makes you a human who is attuned to your feelings. Allow the adversity in your life to show just how much you're learning. Let the small moments of joy, like sprinkling brown sugar over a cobbler, remind you just how far you've come in your healing work. Everything isn't all bad, even when things challenge us or trigger us to grow and expand in new and sometimes uncomfortable ways.

You may think that the text exchange didn't warrant such a big and emotional response. But it was huge for me, someone who has spent countless years in a complicated relationship with her mother. Mainly because every time I think we are taking three steps forward, something happens that causes us to take ten steps back.

I share this story because some things will always need tending to in our healing—even if we thought we were further along in our process. Tender bits of our lives may surface at any given moment, and backtracking is a part of healing sometimes. There is nothing wrong with having to start from scratch, time and time again. Yes, that can sound exhausting. However, reframing our thought process around healing is necessary for our growth and personal development. This is where grace, self-compassion, and self-soothing come into play. At that moment with Erika, after my emotions settled and my sad inner child retreated, I had the tools I needed in that moment to feel better, to feel recentered.

In this next section, we'll focus on tending to self-doubt and fear and work through some practices designed to help you anchor yourself in the healing journey so that when you're pulled back to the beginning of your process, you have the tools to begin again.

TENDING TO SELF-DOUBT AND FEAR

In our walk through healing, there will be many moments of backtracking and uncertainty—moments where self-doubt and fear threaten to derail our process. I wish this weren't the case, but it is. The good thing about having to start over is the lessons we can gain if and when we pay attention. Doing the hard things asked of us when it comes to healing, be it in therapy, guided journaling, or conversations with loved ones or with ourselves, is intimidating. Self-doubt and fear will try to scare us away. But running from what we're scared to see won't make the thing that caused us pain vanish. Dismantling self-doubt and fear isn't easy work and it can feel exhausting if we don't have the right tools at our disposal. The key is to exercise our emotional muscles of compassion, commitment, and courage.

We're going to work together to strengthen those muscles and unpack our fear and self-doubt through writing practice. The invitation here is to start small and work your way up. Often when we are doing this type of introspective healing work, we try to tackle the whole thing at once, instead of bit by bit. At one point, I was the queen of doing this very thing—I thought rushing through my healing process would make it easier, and that speeding things up would allow me more time to move on to the next thing I needed to heal. This wasn't and isn't sustainable. What I failed to realize was that it took years of hurt to get to where I was, and so it will take years, if not a lifetime, of healing. I know none of us signs up to be a work in progress forever, but that is a part of being human that we must lean into.

Rest is an essential part of this journey. Rest gives us a chance to tend to our minds and bodies so that we have the reserves to face self-doubt and fear. While there have been many moments where I've felt depleted from too much healing, taking those much-needed rest breaks to not worry about what's tender, aching, or heartbreaking helped me immensely. My fearful inner voice would try to persuade me not to take breaks, telling me that I would miss something if I did. I resisted taking a break because I doubted that I'd make it back to the work I'd been doing. However, after months and months of running from emotional rest, I convinced myself to trust and believe in how far I'd come. Resting wouldn't ruin that or hinder me from future healing. Choosing to take a step back reminded me to find joy, trust that I was worthy of ease, and embrace the happiness that emerges on the other side of all the hard emotional labor.

More often than not, feelings of overwhelm come from trying to see the final picture in our heads—our "healed" self—with no more work to be done. We rush because we want to be better already. But as you explore this work, I'd like to encourage you to do the opposite. Rushing through the things you need to unpack and rearrange will lead to more frustration and less self-compassion. It can knock you down and distract you from getting up again. I quickly learned that healing doesn't work well when it is rushed. Being impatient will not get you anywhere— trust me, I know this from experience.

This goes for mental and physical healing. If we break a bone, cut ourselves, or bruise a body part, patience is needed to heal, right? The same goes for mental wellness, trauma, and emotional well-being. If we are scarred from a breakup, in agony from childhood abuse, or reeling from poor parental relationships, we need adequate time, care, and tenderness to heal. We cannot speed through the pain—we must sit with it and through it. We must learn to stay in the middle of our hurt so that we can get to the other side of it. Allowing self-doubt and fear to run you off will lead you farther away from the end goal of inner peace, healing, and grace.

Over the years, I also came to realize that I was scared to take my time and be in the middle of my healing because I had no idea what trauma or triggers or past pain points would come to the surface at any given moment. I'm not a big fan of surprises, and this soul work I am committing to doing is indeed surprising. I doubted my ability to handle the big emotions that could meet me at the surface. Learning to take things step by step—and some days, minute by minute—allowed me the space to trust that I could handle taking my time to heal. I realized I didn't have to rush it, but I had to feel it all. And when I couldn't, I had to also trust myself enough to step away from it in order to return with clearer vision, a lighter heart, and an opened mind.

I'm not saying don't be scared—because this work can be terrifying. I'm nudging you not to run away from what scares you on the page. Look at it, and don't doubt that you are capable of healing the tender parts of yourself and your story. This will take a lot of time, practice, and failing. Nevertheless, when you commit to stay with your healing, you manage to learn patience along the way. As you continue to practice staying close to your healing rather than abandoning it when self-doubt emerges, it will become less intimidating. Be patient with yourself and this process. The intention for the healing work you're doing is to remind yourself to stick with it, even when you are caught up in moments of uncertainty and anxiety.

In the next practice, on page 38, you will start unpacking your pain on the page, bit by bit, and identifying where and what hurts, and how you want to feel. This exercise is key to building self-trust, the antidote to self-doubt. When you commit to uncovering your true feelings, you commit to reclaiming your power and standing boldly in your truth.

Healing with Art
Morgan Harper Nichols

I am an autistic woman who writes and makes art. Both were something I started doing just as a way of finding peace in my own life. Before my autism diagnosis, which didn't come until I was thirty-one years old, I lived with the burden of fear, anxiety, and comparing myself to others. My diagnosis helped me better understand myself and learn how to heal.

For most of my life, I've been comparing myself to people around me. And not only how others create or what they do with their lives, but also how people find peace in their lives—how they find resolve. For example, I love to read what other people do to cultivate self-care in their lives. Sometimes I would read a story about someone's healing method or what they're doing to find their way and think, *If I do that, maybe it'll work for me too.* My autism diagnosis gave me a lot of clarity around why certain things were not working for me—like taking a warm bath. That is not calming to me. The water feels weird on my skin, always has, and I never knew why. I used to think, *I should enjoy this. It should make me feel better.* I'd light the candles and do the whole ritual thing. And I'd still be like, *Why don't I enjoy this?* When I received my autism diagnosis, I found out that I also have a sensory processing disorder. Having this disorder makes certain textures feel weird. And even having water touch my skin leaves me feeling extremely uneasy and nervous.

I dealt with a lot of anxiety growing up. My family has a lot of health complications, and family members that I was close to passed away at young ages. I've always felt that life is so fragile. It made me reflect a lot on why I was still here. Like, what was so special about me? I wanted to live a beautiful and meaningful life, especially if it could end abruptly, at any time. I recently realized that I am the age of a deceased family member who I was very close to and saw almost every day. I sat back and thought, *Oh my gosh, I'm the age they were when they died.* When they passed away, it was a holiday, and we were there. I experienced that at eleven years old. To realize they were in their early thirties, and now so am I—I've been struggling with that. I don't really know the words for it other than an overwhelm of anxiety, stress, anger, and grief all mixed together. They're gone, and I am still here—it blows my mind and requires daily acts of healing. Unfortunately, I've had a few other family members pass since then. Each time, I am taken to an anxious place. On one hand, loss makes me grateful for life. And on the other side of things, it does make me wonder what I'm supposed to be doing. I immediately want answers. It's a constant ebb and flow for me.

A lot of my anxiety stemmed from being very hard on myself. I thought I had to figure life out, always do the right thing, and not mess up. But having those good intentions led to more anxiety. I was forcing myself to work through a "be a good human" list and forgetting to take care of myself, which heightened my anxiety. There was a time when I constantly compared myself to others—even when I was just having a bad day. Immediately I would think, *What did I do wrong?*

Receiving my autism diagnosis has helped me better understand my anxiety and fears. I found out that I actually have an enlarged amygdala, which means the fear and anxiety that I feel are heightened. It was so healing to learn that there was something neurological that was out of my immediate control. I have felt fear so heavy since I was a kid. While knowing what was wrong didn't fix or remove the fear, knowing the truth changed my life. I could take a deep breath and offer myself some self-compassion. For years, I put all this responsibility on myself to micromanage the fear that compiles in my head. And now I know this is bigger than me. Coming to terms with that allowed me to see things a bit more clearly.

For the first time in my life, without shame or apology, I decided to take medication. Before being diagnosed, that wasn't something I ever would have seen for myself. I thought I had to figure it out on my own. But now that I know what's actually going on, I've been led to get help on a neurological level. This made a significant difference in my life. Now I extend more grace to myself and do the things that feel healing *to me*, even if I don't see other people doing them.

I'm learning to do what works for me, my sensory process, and my healing. One thing that works for me is taking my medication before showering so that I don't feel as uneasy and uncomfortable the entire time. I have to clean my body, so I have to get through it. And now I feel less stressed that the ritual of bathing and showering just isn't my thing. I know what my thing is, and has been since I was a kid—it's drawing and painting.

When I turned my art into a business, I was convinced for a long time that I had to find a new thing. It was like my art was no longer mine to enjoy but instead something to share and give to others. I felt that I couldn't go to my art as a place of sanctuary anymore. It was almost like I had to go somewhere else to find a deeper connection, something that was not tied to work. But now, I realize it's okay—yes, this is my work—and it's also something that I feel is healing my inner child. When there's stuff going on in the middle of the day, and I'm coloring, I am healing *and* working. That kid part of me, the six-year-old Morgan inside of me, is thrilled about that. So, no matter what, I have to keep that a part of my life, even as it has become work. Answering the call of my creative heart has been life altering. I love making things that mean a lot to me and can connect to others.

Since receiving the autism diagnosis, I feel that I'm learning more about myself and reclaiming parts of myself that I've kind of designated to work, but it's not just work. It's also deep healing and creative freedom. When I start thinking that drawing and painting isn't the ultimate self-care, I remind myself that this is what I need—so I'm going to do it. And I've been really proud of myself for that. It's not a perfect journey at all. I still have days where I'm way too hard on myself, but I'm definitely learning more and more about what I like, what I enjoy, and what I need. I am learning to really own that.

As I heal and know what I need more clearly, I've also been resting more. Emotional rest has been essential for me too. I've grown more comfortable with the world having to wait. My well-being is vital to my survival and my art, motherhood, and commitment to my craft. This has to include rest and recentering. On my emotional healing journey, I've grown to see that I need space. That doesn't mean I'm avoiding things. It means I recognize that I can't hold all of this all the time at full capacity. I have been giving myself more permission to set things aside for a moment and get back to them when I can.

I heal by doing things that remind me that I'm a human being, and in a lot of ways, I'm still that little kid who just wants to feel safe in the world—and who didn't feel safe in the world. I went undiagnosed for most of my life, I dealt with a whole lot, and I didn't know why.

I heal by returning to those things that make me feel safe and make me feel at peace. When I was a little kid, I was so overwhelmed. So I take my power back by finding ease.

I heal by painting.

I heal by doodling.

I heal by going outside and taking my shoes off and letting my bare feet touch the grass and watching the movement of the clouds and looking for shapes.

I heal by looking up at the trees.

I heal in a whole lot of little ways.

Getting back to the little things that I wasn't able to notice before brings me a sense of peace—and now that helps me heal as an adult.

I am healing today by healing my younger self.

Morgan Harper Nichols *is an artist, a writer, and a musician.*

Identifying Pain Points and Feelings

Make three columns in your journal. Title each column with one of these questions: "What hurts?" "Where does it hurt?" "How do I want to feel?" Start with one column at a time. You can write things that are big or small. Whatever you write, make sure you're honest with yourself about your feelings. It doesn't matter whether it sounds silly, insignificant, or too much for the paper to hold. It's never any of those things. Remember, the goal is to be intentional and vulnerable. As you list your words or phrases under each section, pause for a few moments to reflect and read back what you wrote down. Each column should have three to five things. Do not feel rushed to do this practice all at once. Come back to it over the next few days and see what resonates with you the most. Fresh eyes always make the process a bit easier to work through. Once your chart is complete, pick the most resonant thing from each column and unpack it by asking yourself *why* and *how* questions. See the following examples and use them as prompts.

What hurts? > Being laid off from my job. > **Why** does that hurt? > Because I felt blindsided by it and now I'm dealing with feelings of rejection. > **How** do you want to feel? > I want to feel like a valuable part of the next team I am on.

What hurts? > Losing my mother-in-law to breast cancer. > **Why** does that hurt? > Because she was the glue in our family and we miss her beyond words. > **How** do you want to feel? > Even on the hard days, we celebrate her life. We want to feel her presence as often as we can.

What hurts? > Feeling like I was unloved and rejected as a child. > **Why** does that hurt? > Because it still makes me feel inadequate, lost, and alone in adulthood. > **How** do you want to feel? > I want to feel secure in myself and loved in my relationships.

Journaling

Embracing Your Truth

To develop self-trust, we have to tell ourselves the truth. This practice is designed to help you embrace your truth so that you can face self-doubt whenever it arises. To do this, we must be honest about both our fears and our strengths. This is an act of courage and vulnerability. I am inviting you here to identify your fears while affirming yourself with positive and supportive language. Turn to a blank page in your journal and make a T-chart. Label one side "What Scares Me" (fears and self-doubts) and the other side "I Am" (positive affirmations).

When we put things down on paper, we can see our truth in front of us—big or small. Writing things down calls us to be truth tellers in a new way. It encourages us to get up close and personal with ourselves on the page. It's impossible to run, hide, or lie to ourselves.

When I do this exercise, I like to get as real as I can with myself on the page. It can be very uncomfortable, but that discomfort has proven to be extremely helpful in the long run. Why? Because it forces me to look at the things I'd rather not see. It inspires me to look at not only the negative or challenging things in my life but also the positive things, and that gives me the courage to continue on the path I'm on.

My nudge here is not to turn away from the page, but to turn toward it. If you're scared of heights, write that down. If you're scared of abandonment, write that down. If you're scared that you're never going to find love again, or at all, write that down. Nothing is too much or too little, as long as it's your truth.

The lists can be as deep or as lighthearted as you want or need them to be. The only requirement is being unapologetically honest about anything and everything that emerges. Writing to heal is about identifying the small moments of fear, joy, love, and gratitude that emerge. It's not always

Journaling

about the huge mountains we have to climb; our valleys are just as important to explore. Your truth won't always look pretty and done up—and it doesn't have to. Authenticity is seldom wrapped in a beautiful package. We aren't writing to perform a part; we are writing to get real with ourselves and heal. Keep that in mind as you dive into this.

Remind yourself that perfection isn't welcome on the page and that if this feels hard on the first try, it's okay. Keep trying. You do not have to do this list in one sitting; you can make a daily practice out of this exercise. If that feels too intense, think about working on it over the course of ten days, adding two new things to your list a day: one in the fear column and one in the affirmation column.

If you need a nudge, here are some examples from my own journal:

WHAT SCARES ME	I AM
Not being enough	Capable of discovering my worth
Not progressing in my life	Taking steps to move forward in my life
Failing and not being able to recover from it	Learning that failure is a part of growth and success
Dying before living a full life	Alive today and will embrace living in the moment
Being unhappy and not knowing where or how to find joy	Giving myself permission to start over as many times as I need to
Putting the needs of others before mine and feeling burned out	Taking care of myself first so that I have the energy and space to share my abundance

cont'd

Now, when I look back at my list, I am reminded of how far I've come. Some things in my fear column still scare me a little but they're not as resonant as they once were. My affirmations show me that even in fear and doubt, I can be patient, kind, and compassionate with myself and my process. As you work through your lists, remember to release that judgmental voice telling you that you're doing it wrong or that what you're scared of is silly. That voice is lying to you. Getting to the root of your healing will require you to be brave enough to silence that inner critic. The more you do this practice, the more you'll learn how to sit in harmony with the discomfort that may arise. Give yourself permission to be present on the page. Don't rush to get it done. Pace yourself and pay attention to how you're feeling throughout the process.

I Am Making Space

Making space for clarity, rest, and healing will require letting go of thoughts, feelings, and things that weigh us down and keep us stuck. Not everything we've been holding on to can come with us. Letting go is uncomfortable, but keeping a tight grip on what you need to release will harm more than it will help. Self-doubt will not serve us on this journey.

This making-space meditation can be repeated daily as a reminder to give yourself permission to let go of fear and self-doubt before your day begins or after your day ends. You can also pick a line that resonates the most with you, write it down on a sticky note, and keep it somewhere you can see it. I also invite you to think about recording the affirmations and playing them back to yourself when you need them.

Before beginning this meditation, take three deep breaths in through your nose and out through your mouth.

> *In the presence of fear,*
> *I will make space for courage.*
>
> *In the presence of self-doubt,*
> *I will make space for self-belief.*
>
> *In the presence of hurry,*
> *I will make space for slowing down.*
>
> *In the presence of overwhelm,*
> *I will make space for rest.*
>
> *In the presence of overthinking,*
> *I will make space for letting go.*
>
> *In the presence of chaos,*
> *I will make space for inner peace.*
>
> *In the presence of confusion,*
> *I will make space for clarity.*
>
> *In the presence of pain,*
> *I will make space for self-compassion.*

Meditation

OFFERING SELF-FORGIVENESS

Hating yourself is not fertile ground for your healing. You have to forgive yourself for what you did or didn't do, knew or didn't know, as you work through your past and your present. Holding yourself hostage to your mistakes will not make the outcome you experienced any different.

Self-forgiveness creates space for emotional expansion. When we're able to let go and forgive ourselves for things that have caused us pain and suffering or for the mistakes we've made, we're able to create space for growth, and we can start to practice being a more compassionate person for our past and present selves. In turn, of course, we're able to offer that compassion to other people. Healing grants us the opportunity to grow in new ways. Growth is liberating, even when we are greeted with hard things, tough choices, and challenging moments.

Forgiving ourselves is not an easy task. It is complicated, especially when you've dropped the ball, you've hurt someone or yourself, or you think something is your fault. We are flawed humans, and we'll constantly have to work through this practice of not emotionally tormenting and abusing ourselves for the things we cannot change. As you work your way through this book, understand that self-forgiveness is the key to all forgiveness. This is your unique journey, and forgiveness will mean different things along the way as you unpack your trauma and look at your pain points on the page.

When I became a mom at eighteen, I was in an extremely broken and emotionally unhealthy place. I hated myself and was on a path to destruction. But after having my daughter, something clicked deep inside of me. I chose to change for the better to give my daughter the emotional stability and support that I'd never had. I wanted to be the best mother and woman I could be. I wanted to lead by example, and I wanted to move through life with love.

It was hard. No one taught me how to live like that; I had to get lost along the way and figure it out. I had a lot of trouble forgiving myself as I started to mature and heal. As I explored my healing on deeper levels, I made a lot of strides in the right direction, but I was actively avoiding self-forgiveness. It felt too big, too scary, and something I was unworthy of. Even as I did the work to learn about what I needed to heal and what behaviors and thoughts led me to teen motherhood, self-forgiveness remained elusive. Therapy helped me. Journaling was a cathartic outlet for me. Healing started to happen, slowly but surely. However, I was still trying to evade forgiving myself. This was holding me back and stunted my healing.

Finally, at the age of thirty, I hit a breaking point. I found myself feeling very mad and upset for not valuing myself or my body. I felt devasted for my younger self and mad at her for not knowing better. I'd even adopted the harmful habit of blaming myself for the abuse I'd gone through at the hands of people whom I trusted. One day, I broke down. I couldn't take it anymore. With eyes filled with tears, I said to myself, "I am so sorry for everything. I forgive you for everything. I'll love you through this." My path to self-forgiveness—raw, messy, and tender—truly started that day.

One of the tallest mountains I had to climb was learning to forgive myself for the mistakes I'd made in the past and for the wrong choices and decisions that I repeated over and over again. As I embarked on the journey of self-forgiveness, I learned that beginning again would be essential; starting over when I needed to had to be okay. I could not truly heal until I started to truly forgive myself.

My invitation to you here is to lay down the armor of self-hatred. It's not protecting you from anything or anyone. We can't commit to only bits and pieces of the healing work. We heal by committing to the entire process: the good, the bad, the shameful, the sad, and the glorious. You live with yourself every day; it is important that you make space for self-forgiveness. Walk yourself through this work. Step by step. Moment by moment.

Letter to Self

Starting from scratch requires self-forgiveness, and in this exercise you'll practice forgiving yourself. Think about a significant moment in your life that still requires your attention. For example, my letter a few years ago was focused on loving and forgiving my eighteen-year-old self. Maybe you were too hard on yourself for a mistake you made. Perhaps you did something you're ashamed of and haven't given yourself the grace to let it go.

If you're human, it's likely that you've made your fair share of mistakes and poor choices. Or perhaps you have been hurt or mistreated, and you blame yourself for what happened. Dig deep here and see what comes to the surface. I encourage you to be vulnerable and address everything, from your failures to the things you can't and couldn't control to your ability to forgive yourself. Allow every feeling that emerges to be what it will. Be raw, vulnerable, and honest, and then give yourself grace, compassion, and understanding. Close the letter with a promise to forgive and love all the messy and tender parts of yourself, no matter what.

Journaling

Conversation

Lean on a Friend

Doing this healing work alone can be overwhelming and, at times, discouraging. In this practice, you'll connect with a trusted friend or family member. Often we are quick to suggest other people forgive themselves, but we aren't able to practice that in our own lives. Ask a loved one to share their experience of forgiving themselves and others. Then reciprocate by offering your own experiences with and thoughts on forgiveness. Some questions to get the conversation going might include:

What haven't you forgiven yourself for and why?

Name one thing you'd like to let go of as you heal.

Whom do you need to extend forgiveness to so that you can be free from grudges and pain?

What have you forgiven yourself for?

What's the hardest thing about healing and self-forgiveness?

MAKING ROOM FOR NEW BEGINNINGS

Healing requires us to make the hard choice to start over and leave behind what we thought we knew. Deciding to do things differently also challenges us to show up and do the work it takes. We'll see results only when we make a commitment to the work that lies ahead.

There is a lot of talk about manifestation in the wellness space, but very little about the steps we must take to bring what we want to fruition. We cannot just wish things into existence. We must also do the work while we wait. Healing demands effort. We cannot have one foot in the door and the other out. We've got to be all in. Why? Because that is how we heal the whole self—by paying attention to every nook and cranny of suffering, pain, joy, gratitude, and humanness.

Manifestation requires making space for what we want to grow in our lives. There's no magic in manifestation. Yes, we can name things we want and write them down, create a vision board, or record voice memos. That first step of identifying what we want is crucial. However, bringing our longings to fruition also means making intentional space, which requires letting go. We must release in order to receive.

Letting go is crucial for creating the adequate room we need to receive the clarity and lessons of healing. There is absolutely no way around this. If we skipped it, we would miss vital information, such as what we need or don't need, or what we want or don't want. We become increasingly connected to ourselves on the journey when we take the long way. Each step toward healing, transformation, and emotional sustainability holds a stepping stone to the next phase in our growth.

This lesson showed up in my own life a couple of years ago, when I was engulfed in my work, teaching people how to write to heal. I cherish facilitating meditation and breathwork practices. The career I have built for myself is my dream come true until it wasn't. I was having my busiest year ever, and I didn't know how to balance or emotionally handle the growth.

I was doing my best to raise my children with intention, be a loving wife, and nurture my friendships in addition to balancing my dream job. I was failing miserably. My anxiety peaked, my depression hovered, and I felt lost. I had a recurring dream in which I was stuck in the middle of nowhere, alone and terrified. I didn't understand what was happening to me. After all, I'd manifested this life of deep healing so I could help others do the same. I'd prayed for inner peace so that I could clearly see and use my gifts to lead by example. But all of that work was coming undone because my mental health was spiraling out of control.

I was asking, praying, and wishing for change but I wasn't putting any action behind the words. I wasn't taking accountability for the role I had to play in making my experience better. I knew I needed to ask for help and find a therapist. I wanted to start using the mindfulness tools that I had in my back pocket, but they felt so far away and out of reach. Things had gotten so bad that

I began pulling my hair from my scalp—a condition called trichotillomania—to find relief. I hadn't been triggered to pull this bad since my late teens. I was in shambles and having an extremely tough time finding my way back home to myself.

Figuring out how to get back to myself was painful. I struggled, sobbed, and desperately wanted to look for new ways out of my grief and pain because I couldn't fathom having to heal from the ground up again. My therapist at the time kindly said, "You know the deal, Alex. You have the tools. Sometimes starting over is the only way to get back up." It was after that session that I cried until I had no tears left. And then I decided to do the hard thing: begin again. It was time to stop simply wishing for things to get better. It was time to start doing the work to make them better.

I began by making a list of what I wanted to be true, what I'd been avoiding, and the actions I needed to take for healing to start happening. The page is where I not only uncovered my truth but also where things started, finally, to make sense.

My list had things like:

I want to feel *at ease in my mind.* **I've been avoiding** *medication.* **I need to let go of** *that avoidance and ask my doctor what my prescription options are.*

I want to be happier *with where I am in life.* **I've been avoiding** *my gratitude practice lately.* **I need to let go of** *not being present and start paying attention to the beauty in front of me.*

Writing these things down reminded me that I am in control of my life when I am being honest, open, and shameless in the process and with myself. Practicing mindfulness when you're in a highly anxious or emotional place is challenging. I get that; I've been there, and I empathize. It's uncomfortable to redirect our thoughts so that we can start the process of making room for new beginnings, but that is where we learn how to be our own greatest allies.

As we heal, we have to get real with ourselves and stay committed to letting go of the things that are not serving us. If we want to feel good about ourselves and our lives, there will be people, places, things, and habits that have to be shed. We can't just speak words of manifestation and affirmation in the hope that they'll come true; we need to take actionable steps to make them happen. When we stop avoiding facing ourselves head-on, we start showing up in new ways and, hopefully, work toward building the lives we want.

Releasing to Receive

For this practice, you'll ground yourself with your breath as you release what is not serving you. You can do this in one sitting or break it up, whatever feels good for you.

I invite you to get into a comfortable position anywhere that makes you feel calm. This might be in your home, at a park, on your bed, or on the grass.

Read through the practice three times. Return to this breathing exercise as often as you need to feel grounded, centered, and reminded that in order to grow, you have to make space for letting go.

> *(Inhale through the nose.)*
> *In this moment, I am releasing uncertainty to receive peace of mind.*
> *(Exhale through the nose.)*
>
> *(Inhale through the mouth.)*
> *In this moment, I am releasing avoidance to receive clarity.*
> *(Exhale through the mouth.)*
>
> *(Inhale through the nose.)*
> *In this moment, I am releasing rushing to receive the presence of peace.*
> *(Exhale through the nose.)*

Repeat three times, slowly and steadily.

Breathwork

Healing, One Deep Breath at a Time
Glennon Doyle

Alex Elle: Who are you and what do you do?

Glennon Doyle: This question should be easy, but it doesn't feel that way when I think about it. Ten years ago, I would have said, "I'm Glennon Doyle. I am a writer, a mother, a woman, a Christian, and a wife." Over the last ten years, I have found it less comfortable to add anything after *I am*. I've lost many of the identities I used to cling to fiercely. I don't know if I identify as a Christian anymore. I find myself less and less identifying with gender in any way. I read *Untamed* now, and I'm like, *Wow, that's so interesting*. I probably wrote the word *woman* four hundred times in that book. Years later, it's hard to imagine having identified so strongly with the word *woman*. I don't know what it really means anymore. Gender suddenly feels like a made-up thing. When it comes to my sexuality, I don't feel like I identify with gay or lesbian either. I was married to a man and was with men my whole life. And then, when I was forty, I fell in love with Abby. Even with my career as a writer, I haven't really written anything in three years. So as I reflect, I am fairly certain that I am Glennon. Each day, I wake up and try to give and take, and be present with as much love, care, and intention as I can.

AE: Why haven't you written anything lately?

GD: I feel like in the creative life, there's output time, where I'm planting the seeds and making the thing to release into the world. And then things shift, and it feels like a different time where I don't have anything more to give. During my downtime, I started my podcast with my sister and my wife. And what I am finding is that podcasting is much less lonely than writing. Writing is very lonely for me psychologically and mentally because I feel gone. When I think about everything we're taught about peace, joy, and antianxiety being connected to being present, I realize I'm not present when writing a book. I'm just gone. Even when I'm with my family, I feel like I'm still trying to figure out how to get that paragraph right. I'm not paying attention to anybody. My kids refer to this as "Mom being underwater." And when I hear the word *underwater*, I check back in, like, *Wait, I'm here.* I'm not paying attention to anybody because I'm trying to figure out the next frickin' thing I'm going to write.

Pairing that with healing, writing requires me to go places that are not always the most healthy. When I reflect on my shared stories and how I've presented and written about my family—which I'm proud of—I realized I'd been, as Hannah Gadsby describes, pinning them down. Like how scientists pin bugs down so they can study them. As I change and grow, that makes much less sense to me. During this break from writing, I don't know if pinning them down feels right to me anymore. Thinking about my children being in my presence and becoming a story doesn't feel aligned with our trajectory. *Untamed* went crazy, and there was a lot more attention than I'd ever seen before, so maybe it's that. It's interesting that having all of that attention still isn't the answer to living a life that is fulfilled. Right now, my main focus is creating my own idea of what is enough.

AE: How has healing shown up in your life?

GD: The thing that shaped my healing process the most was my addiction. I used to think I was just totally broken because I became an addict when I was ten years old. And so when that happens, you think you were just born broken. I thought healing was something that could fix the brokenness. In my mind, there was a perfect way to be, and I was not that way. Healing for me was more like a fixing. I was trying to get to the state of being whole like I thought other people were. I don't feel that way anymore at all. I don't believe that any of us are broken. We're all sensitive in different ways, and different things hurt us. Maybe healing is not something that takes us from broken to fixed, but from alone to connected or from afraid to peaceful. Realizing this changed things for me. What has ended up healing me the most is being around honest people who will talk candidly about how hard it is to be human—not in a "woe is us" kind of way but in a matter-of-fact, fiercely honest kind of way. I first found this type of honesty in recovery meetings.

AE: Was there something specific or in particular that shaped your healing process?

GD: I remember being in high school and hating being in the cafeteria. It was like *Lord of the Flies* to me. At the time, I was severely bulimic, and I walked into the guidance counselor's office to ask for help because I didn't know how to do life anymore. In doing that, I started to understand that there can be environments that work for everyone else that do not work for me, and I don't have to stay. The way that the world operates can crush a lot of our spirits. We think we have to keep showing up in certain environments, and we have to keep going back to bury ourselves and soldier on. And that day, I learned I could refuse to do that. A part of my healing is remembering that I have agency and freedom to walk out of places that are insulting my soul.

AE: What creative modalities have you used to heal?

GD: Yoga and meditation are really helpful to me. When I feel really lost in anxiety, smells are very important to me—candles and essential oils help me a lot more than is normal. Sound, music, and touch are also healing. I'm absolutely obsessed with coziness—I can't even wear jeans because they feel so oppressive.

AE: How does emotional rest refuel your healing?

GD: The beauty of having had my mental health crises is that I truly learned that my main job is to keep showing up and not lose my shit. There's a lot of care and rest that have to happen for me every single day so that I can keep doing those two things. I spend a lot of time refueling, and I can see the quality of my life when I commit to my spiritual practices and rest. When I show up with people, they can see how attentive, grounded, and present I am.

AE: How do you heal?

GD: One deep breath at a time.

Glennon Doyle *is an author, an activist, and a podcast host.*

REALIZING AND NAMING YOUR NEEDS

There will be challenging moments in your healing practice. Most of these can be linked to identifying how to be clear about your wants and needs. Many of us weren't raised to be aligned and in tune with ourselves. Instead, we were often taught that being selfless and putting the needs of others over our own is how we live a righteous life. While caring for and loving those around us is vital for human connection, there must be a balance between community care and self-care. Being there for others doesn't mean abandoning yourself. You are a part of the equation.

I've realized over the years that a lot of my suffering came from self-abandonment, blurry boundaries, and emotional neglect. Naming my needs felt scary and foreign. I learned growing up that the ultimate sacrifice is running yourself into the ground for others and calling it love. Stating what you needed wasn't polite or welcomed. Relearning how to care for and love myself showed me that I matter and that the people I was in relationships with needed me to matter to myself.

In this section, you will practice identifying what you are longing for. This may feel uncomfortable, but try to welcome ease as you heal into a new version of yourself.

Over time, your needs and wants will change. Your boundaries will shift. Each adjustment is normal and should be met with compassion. Some days you'll know what you want and need, and others, you may not. Practice patience with the process as you figure things out and as you figure yourself out. Nothing happens overnight. We know this. So as you move through this process of figuring things out about yourself on the page, extend yourself gratitude for your effort.

This practice is about cultivating self-trust and self-belief that you are just as valuable as anyone else in your life. Don't just brush by your willingness to show up. That is worth celebrating. Facing yourself on the page isn't easy, and yet, here you are, trying your best. Offer forgiveness to any parts of your story that feel challenging to work through. Negative self-talk will block you from allowing your authentic voice to shine through. Come to the page with no expectation other than being honest. Each step of the process is essential to the end result. Bring everything that you're struggling with to the page. If facing your wants and needs feels too big, all the more reason to unpack it in your journal.

As you take this next step on your journey, remember that you are allowed to name your needs without shame or guilt. Needing something or someone doesn't make you needy. Release the notion that it does. You are allowed to be supported. We get one life and we cannot live it fully if we're constantly shushing ourselves. Playing it small won't save you, and it won't make you feel any better about yourself or your situation. Showing up on the page is your promise to yourself that you will stop shrinking to fit into the lives of others and into boxes that do not belong to you.

Wants and Needs

In your journal, make two separate lists, one labeled "I Want" and the other labeled "I Need." Set a timer for five minutes and fill in the "I Want" column. Then do the same for the "I Need" column. Think about which list felt more challenging, write that down, and reflect on why. Do not overthink what you're writing on the page. Just write without fear and judgment. Center yourself in your writing. You are allowed to matter. Your wants and needs are important. Release the urge to write what you think sounds good. Show up with honesty and truth.

Journaling

Meditation

You Are Worthy

This practice is designed to follow the "Wants and Needs" journaling practice. In a seated position, tune into your breathing. Start taking deep inhales through your nose and exhaling through your open mouth. Thinking about how the previous writing practice made you feel, breathe in the freedom that comes with naming wants and needs, even if it feels challenging. Exhale any thoughts of self-neglect and unworthiness. Continue paying attention to your breathing. Unclench your jaw, soften your shoulders, breathe. Read the following words out loud or in your head:

I can ask for what I need.

I can vocalize what I want.

I am worthy of having my needs met.

I am open to receiving help.

I can show up as my full self.

I am opening to growing and healing.

Befriending Your Fear

As we start to peel back more layers to access deeper healing, we must reframe how we look at fear and address our pain points. Putting our pain on the page and finding ways to self-soothe during moments of anxiety and stress remind us to slow down and be fully present with ourselves and our tenderness. Often, we get so caught up in the pain that we can't access self-compassion. We can't heal if we keep holding ourselves hostage to what we did or didn't do. This work requires acceptance and grace for what we cannot change. How do we move forward and grow through it? We look at our fear, hurt, and sadness, and we face it without contention or judgment. We can hold ourselves accountable without punishing and hating ourselves if we did something wrong in the past or acted out of character.

The same goes for those of us who have experienced mistreatment in the past. Punishing ourselves for the wrongs we've suffered at other people's hands will not serve us. Healing requires that we make room for understanding, kindness, and compassion. No matter your circumstance, you have to look at the things that have broken you down. We cannot ignore our trauma and pain. To start mending, we must commit to seeing ourselves entirely through the eyes of love and worthiness. This will happen and shift the trajectory of our life only when we're ready. There's no rushing the process. When we speed through healing, we miss things and risk leaving ourselves and our truth behind.

When I was ten years old, I had a formative experience with my biological father—an experience that planted a seed of fear in me that would flourish in the decades to come. My father was an on-and-off presence in my life, and whenever he came around chaos ensued. On this particular day, we were in his car on Interstate 495, and he was speeding and steering the car using only his knees. "Daddy, please stop," I said, horrified. He kept accelerating and laughing. My fear and safety meant nothing. "Daddy, please—I'm scared," I begged. He turned the music up and accelerated some more, using his knees to steer. "Please stop," I screamed, tucking my head in between my legs, praying that he wouldn't crash the car on the beltway. I could feel tears welling up in my eyes. I didn't know what was happening or why. He slowly realized that I wasn't having fun, and I could feel the car slowing down.

"I wasn't gonna crash us! I know how to drive," he scoffed. "What, you don't trust me?"

More than two decades later, I am still traumatized by that experience. Aside from my husband, I rarely let even those closest to me drive me places. And when I have, my heart pounds the entire trip. Looking back on that experience makes my stomach hurt and my eyes water. I remember my heart racing. I remember thinking I never wanted to see him again. I remember feeling like he was a dangerous man who didn't care about me. I remember being mad at my mother for letting him take me for the weekend. I remember being scared to death.

So much ran through my mind for weeks and weeks after that experience. I didn't tell my mom because I was asked not to. As a young child, I'd become the gatekeeper of my dad's secrets and lies, whether it was him endangering my life on multiple occasions or the numerous women I had to bounce between when I would visit him. Being an adult reflecting on one of the many traumatizing experiences I had with him, I can see clearly where I learned to be scared of things—of living.

For years, I didn't tell a soul, not even my husband. Ryan would be confused about why I'd be so jittery in the car, and he didn't understand my unspoken fear or feelings of not being safe. It wasn't until writing about it, all these years later, that I started to look at and process the deep pain I carried from that experience. My husband showed me compassion and love when I shared this secret with him. He promised to keep this in mind when he's driving.

Ryan is a great driver and protector. Openheartedly, he listened and assured me that he would keep me and our children safe, always. He gave me a sense of safety and assurance that I didn't have that night my dad and I were flying down the beltway.

My relationship with my biological father continued to be confusing and complicated for many years. When I turned seventeen, I ceased all communication with him to protect myself from his repeated dangerous and traumatizing behavior, both emotionally and physically. I haven't seen him since. I didn't know it back then, but that act of separation was the first time I'd ever chosen myself. It was the first time I put aside my fear of rejection, heartbreak, and shame to decide to do what was best for me. It took years for me to process the parental trauma I'd been carrying close to my chest. Writing is what helped me process and separate my pain from theirs. It's the thing that welcomed me to be sad, angry, upset, and devasted for feeling let down at every turn. But it's also the thing that taught me how to find joy in healing, ease in changing, and forgiveness when putting things down that never belonged to me in the first place.

I never told anyone about that night in the car with my dad because I didn't want to get him in trouble. I didn't want to hurt him—him hurting me was enough. The lie I'd been taught to swallow was that I don't matter. That made me terrified of existing. I learned in childhood how to shut up and sit down. I learned how to protect the adults around me with my silence by shrinking into my seat. It was second nature to ignore my feelings because

I felt like I didn't exist. Addressing this secret fear—of driving, of danger beyond my control—on the page was my first step in remembering that I don't have to be scared anymore. That I wasn't a little girl pleading with her head tucked between her legs, begging to be kept safe. I reclaimed my power by putting down this fear, looking at it, talking about it, and choosing to befriend it. It was then that I felt liberated enough to say:

Dear Self,

You are safe now. There's nothing to be scared of anymore. I got you.

IDENTIFYING YOUR FEAR ON THE PAGE

No matter how hard we try, we cannot ignore our pain. When it comes to healing what hurts, we have to look it in the face and say, "Come closer." Identifying what aches and breaks us is step one. Committing to putting it down, one piece at a time, on the pages of our journals is how we learn to not only look at ourselves, but also love ourselves. Writing to heal welcomes us to start where we are. Being flawed in this practice, not knowing which way to turn, is how we get comfortable learning along the way. Facing our fear and befriending it requires trial and error. It will be uncomfortable to look at some things you've hidden so that you can function and feel safe. You won't always get it right. You won't always want to do this work, and that's okay. Getting lost along the way may be a fundamental part of this process. Taking breaks as you break through to new levels of healing is necessary for restoration. As you're writing through things, remember that it's impossible to get the answers you desire if you're rushing. To do this work, you have to slow down. You have to take your time and be mindful.

To dive deeper into your healing process, you'll be answering some questions in this section that you may not want to face. I know it's easier to look away, but if we don't start looking at the things that scare us away from ourselves, when will we be able to heal and find liberation in that healing? Befriending your fear is how you start to embody true transformation.

Writing through your fears will require trial and error. One day you may be really into your writing practice and feeling like you're tapping into the root of your pain. The answers may be right there in front of you, making you feel like you're getting closer to finding a way to mend. And then you catch yourself in a slump or question why you're even trying to figure this all out. Stick with it. Every feeling, emotion, and thought is welcome—think of them as your guardian angels inviting you to dig a little deeper. Be kind and gentle with yourself during this process. This soul work isn't supposed to be pretty. It's supposed to be honest, raw, messy, and authentic work. Remember that as you welcome fear into your space, as you extend a hand of friendship, as you surrender, knowing that you are worthy of grace. Know that you can take a step back. Trust that you can find your answers step by step. Engaging with your fear in this way makes room for self-compassion and empathy.

What Are You Scared Of?

Now, it's time to unpack what you're scared of so that you can begin to befriend your fear. In your journal, answer the following questions:

What fear has been coming up for you the most these days?

What is your first memory of this fear?

How is it getting in the way of your healing?

What would it feel like to befriend this fear and make it part of your healing?

Journaling

Sitting with Fear

Find a quiet, comfortable place to sit. Close your eyes and think about what fear has taught you about healing. Are you running from your fear or welcoming it in? As you reflect, remind yourself to hold intentional safe space for whatever comes up. It's easy to get caught up in a whirlwind of judgment and self-criticism. It's easy to shut down when fear arises. That will not serve you in this practice, nor will it make you less scared of whatever you're tackling. Remember, you don't have to figure it all out today. Know that the practice of befriending our fear takes time and effort. Take things slowly and resist the urge to rush the process of moving through what may be frightening. The more you do this practice, the less scary your fears will be. When we bring our attention to our fears again and again, they begin to lose their power.

Meditation

SEEING PAIN AS A PARTNER

Sometimes the healing we have to do feels more painful than the thing that hurt us to begin with. I know that may feel discouraging, but the invitation here is to welcome every emotion so that you give yourself room to flourish. Changing, healing, and growing stretches us emotionally and sometimes physically. And while it may feel easier to turn away and not bother mending the bruised and broken parts of you, what good will that do in the long run? Staying stuck in our pain will rob us of our joy and leave us feeling incapacitated and hopeless. We commit to healing by doing the hard things it takes to create a sense of ease in our lives.

Choosing to address our healing head-on is a self-nourishing act; it is an invitation to choose yourself, even when things hurt like hell. Being open to the possibility of healing is to welcome the light after your darkest days. Something that continues to support me as I heal is looking at my pain as a partner rather than an enemy. This reframe took years to cultivate, but it's shown me the duality in accepting what is, what was, and what I can and cannot change. Pain can be a pathway to growth. When I became open to the idea of that, I was able to pace myself and look at my suffering for exactly what it was. No judgment. No frills. No sugarcoating. Healing is not one-size-fits-all. Allowing the process to ebb and flow is how we start to evolve emotionally. Trying to be the perfect healer who escapes future struggle will not serve you. It's important that we learn to look at our healing through a neutral lens. I know, that's easier said than done. However, when we explore that practice without bias, we get closer to the fact that we may need to heal from things more than once.

A few years ago, I had a really hard time processing some of the pain from my childhood. I'd just started therapy again, and talking about things I'd suppressed sent me into a spiral of emotions. I was convinced that I'd already done the healing work around childhood trauma. Facing it again seemed to be more destructive than helpful. At the time it felt like I'd done enough and I didn't want to go back to that dark place of unearthing. It was then that I realized healing, for me, would be a forever process. That starting over, and sometimes from scratch, would be a part of my journey. Learning how to face my healing head-on, each time a trigger emerged, was going to show me something new about myself, my life, and my healing journey. Don't get me wrong, this wasn't fun. And if I'm being honest, it was aggravating. "Why do I have to heal over and over again?" I would ask my therapist. I would have to find the answer on my own. There was nothing she could say to make it make sense.

The journey to inner clarity around healing is deeply personal. One of my key takeaways from healing head-on is to intentionally rest—i.e., give myself a break. It was hard not to get addicted to the constant pull of self-improvement. Healing and action, to create the life we want, also requires slowing down and resting. Our culture praises knowing what we're doing and where we're going. A lot of us feel lost and disoriented because of this conditioning. Trying to heal as fast as we can, and without emotional breaks, is destructive. Many of us are not healing because we refuse to slow down and sit with the hurt, confusion, and turmoil that we're carrying.

There is deep meaning in the intentional pauses that we take to look at ourselves, and be with ourselves. I understand how intimidating this is. I've been there. However, emotional rest is where we can find transformative healing right in front of us. We have to unlearn being afraid of ourselves. If we refuse to find peace in pausing, breaking cycles and healing our hearts will continue to feel far away. You are not behind for choosing to rest as an act of healing. Trust your inner knowing and the call to slow down.

As much as I wished healing were easier, things can be only what they are. At times, we will be pissed and discouraged that we are back in places we thought we'd healed from. This may cause feelings of uncertainty to arise, but do not be swayed by the backtracking. Each step forward and backward is how we ground ourselves and learn to meet our healing head-on. In those moments, we find a deeper connection to ourselves and the pain we carry. Being a student in this healing process is valuable. Stay committed to finding ease in the midst of the hard and heavy stuff.

Share Your Fear

When we speak our fears out loud and share the stories behind our pain, we can lessen the power they have in our lives. As you become better acquainted with your fear, reach out to a trusted loved one to share your truth. Then ask them if they have any fears they want to share with you. Consider this an exercise of trust, community, and honesty. When we make space to listen, we create a safe environment to share openly with each other. This exercise can feel big and scary, but when vulnerability emerges in the presence of compassion, empathy, and care, it becomes easier to look at what scares us and lean in closer to see what it's trying to teach us.

Conversation

The Duality of Healing and Pain

Pain and healing go hand and hand, and viewing them as partners in our process allows us to recognize how they work together to help us grow.

I invite you to identify the duality of your healing and pain for this writing exercise. In your journal, draw a Venn diagram using two overlapping circles, one labeled "Pain" and the other "Healing." Fill each of the circles and their overlapping space with words that each one can feel like for you.

Trying to figure out where to place the words can feel intimidating, but my nudge here is to not overthink and just write. It may be helpful to start with a brain dump. Put things wherever, without too much intention or thought. And then as you go through the writing practice, you can go back and move words around. You can cross things out, erase things, or even have one word in all three sections. There is no right or wrong way to begin. You just have to start.

Here's an example of this exercise from my journal. Feel free to pull any words from it that resonate with you.

Journaling

PAIN CAN FEEL LIKE

THEY BOTH
CAN FEEL
LIKE

HEALING CAN FEEL LIKE

grief
guilt
loss
unresolved trauma
heartbreak
depression
conflict with loved ones
rejection
physical injury
anxiety
shame
self-hatred
negative self-talk

lessons
new beginnings
growth
a journey
a myth
an adventure
a challenge
self-discovery

relief
joy
peace
wholeness
fulfillment
love
freedom
understanding
compromise
boundaries
unity
self-choosing
acceptance

Leaving Space for Healing
Megan Rapinoe

I'm a very passionate person. I grew up in a big family, so I love having people around. My family is the type that will help anyone. They will give you the shirt off their back if you need it. I try to be that way as well. I love to have a sense of humor. I'm sure that being self-deprecating, paired with my humor, is how I cope with certain things, but laughter is a big part of my life and how I connect. I do my best to live by the principle that we get only one life and we should cherish our time here.

For the most part, my childhood was wonderful. But when I think of the healing I've done, it's often connected to my older brother's drug addiction. Something that always lingered in the background was his struggle. His addiction started when he was fifteen, and because of that, he's been in and out of the criminal justice system most of his life. I remember being ten years old, trying to grasp what was going on. I understood some of what was happening, but there were also a lot of unknowns. Anyone who has a family member struggling with addiction of any kind knows that a lot comes with it—a lot of hurt, pain, and confusion.

One thing that has helped me heal over the years is how open and honest my family has always been about my brother's addiction. They never hid anything from my sister and me. His addiction was never something that we were made to feel ashamed of or embarrassed by. We were all doing the best that we could to deal with and process what was happening.

My parents encouraged us to communicate openly and find people who could support us. They never pretended that the addiction didn't exist, even when they were unsure how to handle it. Their ability and decision to be transparent and vulnerable made a world of difference. It diffused the shame, secrecy, and stigma that so many people end up carrying when faced with addiction.

It wasn't always easy. There were times when I struggled with things and had to sort through them on my own. Processing on my own time helped me learn more about addiction and the criminal justice system. It also showed me how to be a lot more empathetic and heal from some things that hurt me when I was younger. I'd been so confused about why this was happening, and I used to question why he was hurting us. Once I got to a place of acceptance, understanding, and empathy, many things became more apparent to me. Talking about everything we were facing left space for those questions and made room for healing.

Not pushing my pain and sadness away allowed me to feel all of my feelings, which helped me understand that addiction isn't just a choice everyone makes every day. As I matured, I realized that my brother didn't just wake up *wanting* this for himself. He didn't enjoy a life that revolved around hurting me and everyone around us. Addiction is a disease. Realizing this made room for me to address my healing head-on. I was being called in to think about his addiction from his perspective. Then I was able to think about how it was impacting the whole family and how we could support him while being empathetic and having boundaries.

I walked through an entire range of emotions when it came to accepting what and how things were. A key learning was to be okay in knowing that I can't change anyone or make them do something they don't want to do. Having this very real and emotionally complicated experience showed me the possibilities of healing individually and as a unit. We weren't hiding or ashamed. We were actively and collectively doing our best to heal and be in tune with our emotions surrounding our loved one's internal struggles.

I'm grateful that my brother's addiction wasn't hidden from us. It was out in the open, and we addressed it as a family. Even when I was young, I don't think keeping this a secret would've been supportive for any of us. Secrets and shame prevent you from moving on. They prevent you from seeing things from different perspectives.

As a professional athlete, I've learned so much about balancing my emotional and physical health over the years. When I take a step back and look at my life professionally and personally, I realize the importance of seeing things from different viewpoints. Having dealt with my brother's addiction for so many years, I became skilled in looking at things in life from all angles. Something I started paying closer attention to in 2020, during the pandemic, was doing less, but doing it better—partnered with not spreading myself too thin. Even when it's hard for me at times, not doing anything can feel best.

I learned to be okay with having nothing on my plate some days. I think that was a point of healing for me too. Giving myself permission to be at home with no plans and a good book taught me to slow down. I started intentionally relaxing. Doing nothing and having a lot more time to myself showed me that I needed exactly that. Being able to sit with my thoughts is the break I need. I love people, I'm very social, and I enjoy working. So pressing pause isn't my first option, but I know it's necessary and helpful in the long run.

Reminding myself that overworking is not the point of life brings me back to the moment. Reflecting on the role that healing plays in my life, I feel that I heal by being in my home with my fiancée, by taking time out just for myself as the whole goal. I heal by seeing friends and family; connecting with them fuels me. Meaningful connections and relationships show me that I am seen as my authentic self, which brings me back to life. No matter what I've been through or walked through, be it my brother's addiction or trying to find balance in taking care of myself, I am reminded that there's so much happening around me. I am not the most important thing going on, which makes me feel really grounded and mindful about life as a whole.

Megan Rapinoe *is a professional soccer player and captain of the US national team.*

CULTIVATING POSITIVE SELF-TALK

As we work on befriending our fear, we have to balance that work with positive self-talk. Affirmations—positive, uplifting phrases that can be repeated out loud or in my head—play a major role in my work and life. I am a big believer in being kind to ourselves, especially when we are at the rock bottom of our lives. How we treat and speak to ourselves matters more than we realize. Positive self-talk is essential to changing our behavior, cultivating self-compassion, and being kinder, more patient, and less judgmental.

We tend to learn a lot of our self-talk, both good and not so good, while growing up, even before we are able to do, think, and feel for ourselves. Sometimes what we end up carrying emotionally is not even our baggage or truth to begin with; they are figments of other people's ideas and thoughts. External projections can come from our care-takers, coaches, teachers, or friends.

Looking back and analyzing who taught you how to speak to yourself and be in the world can reveal a lot. It can also nudge you to move forward and evolve for the better. Speaking and acting on positive self-affirmations is an invitation to reclaim your voice, truth, and power without seeking validation from others. This is why affirmations are important to emotional growth and mental wellness. We are invited to look deep within and ask: *Who am I? What do I want? Why am I valuable?*

I love to teach people how to use affirmations to create healthy action in their lives. But often folks think that if they write and say their affirmations, they'll simply come to pass because they prayed on it or put it out in the universe. From my experience, it doesn't work that way. Bringing our affirmations to life requires more than releasing them in your journal to reap the benefits. I wish it were that easy.

Remember, affirmations are just the first step in a manifestation practice. Affirmations without action will keep you stuck. Over and over I've heard elders in my life say, "Faith without works is dead" (James 2:26). And it's so true. So as we do this soul work, we can't just hope and wish and have faith that our affirmations will become the truth. We have to work for it while we wait for it.

Putting action behind your affirmations will change how you look at your capability to overcome, persevere, and grow through the tough times that arise. Affirmations backed by action can shift the path of your life for the better. How? By using them to uncover your personal *why* and *how*. When approached honestly and without judgment, affirmations can be a way to nurture yourself. Quieting your inner critic and learning to hit mute on negative self-talk will require you to get curious about yourself, the words you're using, and the emotionally healthy life you say you want to create. This is always challenging, but I'd like to normalize looking at our challenges in life as a teacher. Facing our challenges is a process that can bring us ease and gratitude.

It's important to note that every day we may be a slightly different version of ourselves. If your affirmations shift and change day to day, that is fine. You are evolving, and this is not a linear practice. Don't hold yourself hostage to perfection. Flaws are welcome in this practice. Find fluidity and be okay with being a constant work in progress.

As you show up on the pages of your journal, you will be stretched and tried at every turn to peel back your layers and get to the root of your truth. Staying committed to self-compassion will allow you to dig deeper into being your best self as well as the person you needed growing up. Allow your affirmation practice to comfort the inner child in you. Affirmations give you the space to mentor your younger self and shift the narrative of your life. And while we can't literally go back and change the past, we can start to heal some of our emotional wounds by inviting ourselves to be the safe space we need.

Journaling

Creating Your Own Affirmations

Self-inquiry is vital to uncovering who we are, what we want, and how we need to grow. In this practice, your affirmations will come from a specific series of questions that I want you to answer openly and honestly. When answering these journal questions, use positive **I am** statements, even if that comes from redirection. The goal is to recenter and build a practice of positive self-talk, even during adverse or challenging experiences. The thought starters below are micro-level, back-to-basics questions that will support you in identifying who you are, what you want, and what you're aiming for as you heal.

Who am I today?

How am I changing?

How am I exercising self-worth?

How am I learning to trust myself?

See my examples that follow.

Q: Who am I today?

A: I am a person who is healing and learning how to become the best version of myself.

Q: How am I changing?

A: I am changing the way I speak to myself under pressure. I am practicing more self-compassion and patience.

Q: How am I exercising self-worth?

A: I am starting to match my words and actions more by not settling in moments of uncertainty.

Q: How am I learning to trust myself?

A: I am learning to trust myself by letting go of control and exploring the different paths that present themselves to me.

When you've finished this exercise, you'll have a list of your very own **I am** affirmations that you can return to again and again. Speak these powerful affirmations out loud when you are facing your fears or when the pain of the journey feels overwhelming.

Cultivating Self-Worth in the Face of Fear

For this meditation practice, I invite you to sit quietly and tune into your breathing and slowly read the following script. Once each sentence is complete, pause and take a deep and slow inhale, then a long, intentional exhale, filling up your belly on the in-breath and emptying it on the out-breath. Mindfully reading through this meditation practice will give you the time and space to absorb and internalize these words. Don't worry too much about believing everything as your truth today. Instead, each sentence may be a work in progress for you. Welcome the possibility of these words being true as you heal, transform, and grow.

I trust that I am valuable. I am standing in self-worth, unswayed by negative self-talk and doubt. I am discovering more confidence, bravery, and meaning in my life. I am faithfully showing up to take care of myself. I will lean into the belief that I am worthy of good, healthy, and whole relationships and experiences. Believing that I am valuable isn't always easy. Still, I am committed to doing my best and being a work in progress. Even when life is uncomfortable and challenging, I vow to stay close to my worth as I move through the world. I trust that self-value allows me to live a full life overflowing with healthy, loving relationships and fulfilling experiences.

Meditation

Preserving Joy
Nedra Glover Tawwab

Alex Elle: Who are you and what do you do?

Nedra Glover Tawwab: I feel like I am so many things to so many people, including myself. And it's always really hard to come up with a good one for this question because I'm constantly shifting. Part of who I am is a therapist. I'm also a mom and a partner. I'm a friend, a daughter, a cousin, and a gardener. I am so many different things in different capacities, and I'm constantly changing and evolving as time goes on.

AE: How has healing shown up in your life, and was there something specific or in particular that shaped your healing process?

NGT: So many things have shaped me along the way, and I think we don't even know we need to heal until we're triggered by something. That trigger is what starts the journey of true healing. When I became a mom, it opened up a space to more deeply evaluate my relationship with my mother. I thought I'd already done a lot of my healing work—until I got pregnant. Pregnancy requires so much sacrificing and unlearning. It was a very interesting process of learning the practice of grace. It is hard to parent without giving yourself grace. Pregnancy and motherhood opened me up and allowed me to discover how to give my parents the same grace I'd started giving myself. Our situations were very different. My mother was a single parent, and I am not. And so, I realized that I had to be grateful for the privilege of having a partner to help me parent and how not having that, in my mom's case, can shape your experience as a parent and how you raise your children.

AE: What events in your life shaped and impacted you to do the most healing?

NGT: As a therapist, I feel like I'm constantly healing because things are always coming up that I need to attend to that I didn't even know about. It's like, *Oh, there's a new thing that needs your attention.* So much of the work that I have to do is still being uncovered. I mean, I know the big stuff, but I think there are so many micro things that are major as well. They're constantly unfolding as things come up in our lives. You may not know that you have an issue with grieving until you have to grieve. You don't know that you have an issue with most things until you're in that position and facing something triggered, and it's like, *Oh wow, I'm impacted by this.*

Sitting with people as they move through different areas of their life, I've learned just how human and connected we all are. We feel like so much of what we experience is different from those around us. And things may come in various forms; grief is grief, hurt is hurt, trauma is trauma. It could be accident trauma, or Daddy-left-me trauma, but the end result is still that trauma. As I listen to people talk about different issues, I learn that much of everything we talk about is relatable. That is because the core feelings of sadness, hurt, and grief are there. It further helps me realize how complicated we are and how connected we are. We are resilient. We are constantly growing, and there's always something that we need to grow from and talk about. It is just a tremendous process to witness.

I think the most impactful thing that I see is adults talking about childhood. Hearing people talk about their child-hood gives me the privilege to be the parent that my kids would need. I hear these adult children talking about their upbringing. I think about how I'm an adult child. I feel grateful to be in a beautiful position to create something different because I am constantly hearing from adults and thinking of my own issues.

AE: What creative modalities have you used to heal?

NGT: I garden. Throughout the years, I've learned that gardening teaches you a lot about letting go—that everything has a season and everything has a cycle. You cannot grow stuff whenever you want to. You have to wait until the ground is fertile. You wait until it is time to grow something. You cannot plant tomatoes in ten-degree weather. You just can't do it. I can't be upset when other people in the world can grow tomatoes when I can't—I mean, I could be upset, but I've chosen not to be. Gardening reminds us that this may not be the time or season for us, but there will be a time, *and* we have to wait. Looking at things through this lens shows so much about who we are as humans and the importance of practicing patience. Because when we want things and it's not our time or season, we must wait. Gardening is a great teacher when it comes to acceptance, healing, and being creative with what we have. It teaches us to preserve the goodness of things and preserve the joy we have in our lives.

AE: How does emotional rest refuel your healing?

NGT: This goes back to pregnancy for me. I was over-functioning in unhealthy relationships before I had children. Having kids woke me up to the energy I was dispensing. I no longer felt like it was appropriate giving that energy away. I cut out a lot of things that were draining my energy because I needed to preserve it for the people in my house. Looking back, emotional rest was helpful because I realized I could do *anything* I wanted, but I couldn't do *everything* I wanted. I had to be clear that I was doing a little bit of everything. I wanted to be more intentional about the health of my relationships and not just have them. You can be a relationship collector and have a lot of stuff going on, or you can have some quality relationships. About eight years ago, I switched from having a higher quantity of relationships to having higher-quality ones. Emotional rest and boundaries gave me the space to be clear about what I wanted and needed.

AE: How do you heal?

NGT: I heal by writing. I heal by being in relationships with people. I heal by focusing on my relationship with myself and by helping other people heal.

Nedra Glover Tawwab *is a therapist, an author, and a relationship expert.*

SELF-LOVE, ONE DAY AT A TIME

We hear a lot about "self-love" these days. People throw the phrase around lightly. But self-love is not a trend or a gimmick. When I was first on my self-love journey, I remember it being talked about in a very whimsical way. It almost felt like I would never achieve it because the images of self-love that I saw felt unattainable. That changed over the years, and I started to see loving myself as just that—practice. Sometimes that practice is messy and complicated; other times, it's easy and lighthearted. I am a firm believer that the act of loving ourselves is sacred and requires us to keep at it daily. Lean into the idea that it's hydrating. It's a force in our lives. A lifeline, if you will. At the end of the day, we live and die with ourselves. Creating a loving inner world is monumental. As you work through this section of the book, I'd like you to remember this guiding affirmation and write down:

I deserve my own love.

Self-love is a steady incline.

Have patience and be easy with yourself. Hating yourself for not learning how to love yourself won't get you to your end goal. As with anything, this healing journey of self-love will ebb and flow. Self-love is a restorative practice. It must be. Reframing our ideas around what it means to be in a safe and supportive relationship with ourselves truly is a teaching moment. With patience and grace, I've found that the love I have for myself gets better with time as I mend.

Everything works hand in hand on this journey. You are allowed to show up for yourself unapologetically. You are going to fall short while doing this work. Remember, perfection isn't welcomed here. Flaws show us who we are and where there is room for clearer self-awareness. A lot of us measure where we are today by our pasts. Whether your past served you well or caused you to struggle, it doesn't dictate your worthiness. You are worthy of good things and self-love no matter what you've walked through in the past. Release the urge to hold yourself hostage to something you cannot change. How will you love yourself through the bad and the good? They both deserve your full attention.

I realized self-love was foreign to me when I went to therapy for the first time. My therapist asked, "What do you love about yourself?" She slid me a piece of paper, set a timer for ten minutes, and told me to make a list. My palms started to sweat, my throat got dry, and I felt entirely out of my comfort zone. I didn't know how to answer that question. What felt even more devastating was that I couldn't access memories of ever feeling truly loved by other people. My mother wasn't affectionate or affirming when I was growing up. Because of the stressors she had looming in her life, most of what I saw and felt from her was rage. My biological father was in and out of my life and extremely harmful whenever he was around. For most of my life up until age twenty-three, I was constantly searching for love outside of myself because I felt like the people who were supposed to love me most didn't.

There were no examples for me to look to. The blank page I was looking at seemed like it was getting blanker and blanker. My eyes started to burn. Time was running out. My therapist looked at me without judgment as I tapped the pen on my forehead. I looked at her and shrugged. "I don't have an answer for this," I said, wholly defeated.

That was the longest ten minutes of my life. The question had unlocked some of my deepest pain. I'd never seen the love of self or others demonstrated. It was foreign. I wasn't taught how to love myself at school, and I did not learn the importance of loving myself in my home. If anything, I connected with self-hatred. I just knew I was doomed.

"It's okay, Alex. All is not lost. I am proud of you for thinking about it even if nothing came up," she said compassionately.

I blinked, stunned by her kindness and a little scared because I knew I was going to have some major home-work to do after that appointment.

Even when we don't know where to begin, we have to start somewhere. My homework from my therapist was to, instead, make a list of what I *wanted* to love about myself. This felt easier than the initial exercise. There were a lot of things that I wanted to love, and putting those things down was a stepping-stone, for me, in the right direction.

Self-Love Stepping-Stones

This exercise is a favorite of mine. It is an invitation to look at how and what you need to love yourself, one step at a time. Think about the the healthy steps you'd like to create or the rituals you'd like to start to cultivate a deeper self-love relationship.

When we allow ourselves to get comfortable with not knowing and are open to figuring out the steps we'd like to take to learn what we want, the practice begins to feel less intimidating and more empowering. You don't have to know all the ways you love yourself today. Some of you will read this and find ease, and others will feel unsure. There is room for both. Once you have created your own stepping stones, you can return to them to deepen your self-love practice. Mine are below as an example.

Not settling for less

Honoring self-boundaries

Holding myself accountable

SELF-LOVE STEPPING-STONES

Clarity around what I want and why

Not ignoring my pain and being honest about it to those close to me

Self-forgiveness and allowing myself to heal without judgment

Journaling

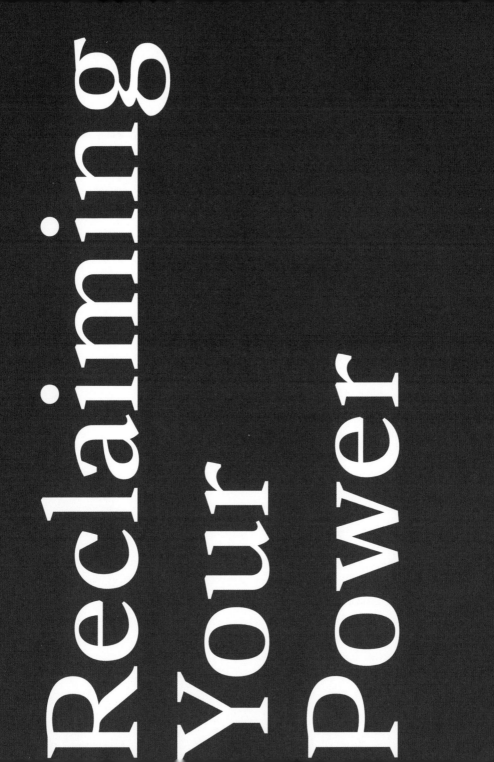

Reclaiming Your Power

Once we have the tools to start from scratch and face our fears, we are ready to reclaim our power. Journaling allowed me to rewrite my story. It showed me exactly what I needed to shift, change, and let go of. Everything I needed to learn appeared vividly on the pages of my journal. When I learned how to write to heal, it became clear that I couldn't hide from myself anymore.

I spent years stuck in a tired, old narrative, avoiding my pain and shame, to the point that it started to make me sick. My anxiety skyrocketed, my depression clawed at me daily, and I didn't know how to fix my broken heart. I was angry. I felt that life had dealt me a crappy hand and I was left to figure it out on my own. Therapy started to not help as much as it once had. I felt like I was replaying my trauma over and over again without gaining the new tools I needed to take control of my life. I didn't know what else to do but write. One day, I grabbed my journal and wrote the questions: *What's hurting you? Where do you feel the most pain? How do you want to feel?* The floodgates opened and I made a list of everything that was aching and longing to be addressed.

We are meant to walk in our truth and purpose. But no one teaches us to ask ourselves the hard questions. We're encouraged to seek the answers outside of ourselves. Go to therapy, and the therapist will heal you. Go to God, and your prayers will be answered. Do meditation, and the answers will come. Go everywhere but inward to find your answers. External support is important and necessary, but it is one step in the direction of healing, not the end of the road. Only you can set yourself free.

Reclaiming my power as I began to heal and get to know myself meant no more shrinking and silencing my voice for the comfort of others. No more pretending that my anxiety wasn't eating me alive. No more making excuses about not taking my healing seriously. It also meant asking myself the questions that I expected others to have the answers to. The best teachers and gurus will tell you that you won't find what you're looking for if you don't get curious about what you want and need. Remembering that you are your own greatest teacher is invaluable.

I was tired of living out a painful story. I was not living a life that was fulfilling, but I wanted to be. I knew I needed to change. I was tired of suffocating and trying to be everything to everyone and nothing to myself. Self-abandonment isn't an act of love. It's a sign of weak boundaries and it can lead to burnout and self-destruction.

My therapy sessions, meditation, and prayers were not enough to sustain the healing work I said I wanted. They fell short because after the venting and unpacking in therapy, I was on my own. Because after the stillness on the meditation cushion, I was back into the grind of life. I was lacking mindfulness and intention because, in reality, I thought I didn't matter and my pain was too potent to heal. I was slacking on doing the work while I was waiting for change to happen because I figured with time things would change.

But as I learned firsthand, healing requires full dedication and commitment. Time isn't the thing that will heal us; practicing what we are learning on and off the cushion, in and out of the therapist's chair, will. I was being nudged through my writing practice to identify how I wanted to show up and be big in my life. Writing revealed where I needed to take action to reclaim my power. I had to commit to making myself a priority, and to stop abandoning myself as an act of love to those around me.

Often, when we are unpacking our emotional suitcase and uncovering the trauma, unhealthy habits, broken boundaries, and pain points we've ignored, it feels too overwhelming. It's almost like we may be better off not unpacking it at all. On multiple occasions, I've found myself not having the mental space and zipping the baggage right back up. Looking at our pain makes it real, and I know it can feel terrifying, but healing starts when we make the choice to face what frightens us most.

Reclaiming our power means holding our fears, pain, hopes, and dreams all at once. We must learn to embrace turning toward the things we've shoved away. Those things are part of our story, but they are not the whole story. We are more than that. This soul work doesn't need us to be strong; it inspires us to be open to possibility. So often we are taught to suck it up, push the pain down, and suppress our feelings, thoughts, and emotions. Releasing that unhealthy way of engaging with our pain is where we can start dismantling the idea that we have to be perfect and put together at every turn.

Life is messy, and so is being human. Healing doesn't require the performance of perfectionism. Instead, it welcomes you to put down the pain you're carrying, hold space for it, and look at it bit by bit. In doing so, joy, ease, and self-love start to emerge. Everything takes time, especially when looking closely at what hurts, what's not serving us, and where we need healthier habits with ourselves and others. Remembering that we all deserve to take up intentional space in this life is how we stand tall and reclaim our power. Settling is no longer the safest option. Showing up fully in your healing is what will set you free and start the new chapter that you're looking for.

UNCOVERING YOUR TRUE VOICE

Uncovering our true voice, our deepest feelings and desires, is our birthright. When we learn to connect with this voice we can better identify where in life we feel silenced, small, or like we're settling. Self-reflection on the page encourages us to ask more questions and unpack our answers. Asking myself the following questions prompted me to get up close and personal with some of my buried trauma and pain.

What is hurting you?

Feeling like I don't matter.

Being stuck and not knowing what to do or where to do it.

Feeling sad about being born to two hurting parents.

Feeling like I can't move far enough away from my past mistakes.

Where do you feel the most pain?

In my chest and jaw.

In my marriage; it feels hard to be vulnerable, even though I feel safe with my husband.

In my back. When I get too stressed, it aches.

In parenthood; sometimes I feel so lost and uncertain. No one taught me how to raise and love other people.

How do you want to feel?

I want to feel confident.

I want to feel safe, even in the face of vulnerability.

I want to feel held, even when people don't understand my pain.

I want to feel a deeper connection to myself.

Turning to what I now call "restorative writing" invited me to take my time and be patient with myself. Restorative writing continues to help me uncover my true voice and take small, intentional steps in the direction of self-liberation. Once I'd written out my answers, I went back and used *why* and *how* questions to dig even deeper, further unpacking the feelings and truths behind each of my initial responses. For example, to unpack my first answer, I wrote the following:

What *is hurting you?*
Feeling like I don't matter.

Why *is this hurting you?*
Because feeling like I don't matter keeps me stuck in cycles that are hard to break away from. Feeling like I don't add value to the world makes it hard for me to remember my worth.

How *do you want things to change?*
I want to be self-reliant when it comes to knowing my worth. I want to build confidence that cannot be broken by rejection, shame, or guilt. I know that recognizing self-worth is an inside job. I will start writing down and reminding myself of the value I bring to the world.

These examples are just the tip of the iceberg in discovering my true voice. Slowly chipping away at layers of self-protection allows for transformation. Identifying your *why* and acting on the *how* is when things start to click and take on new shape. We are the only ones who have the answers to our wants and needs. Even when it feels hard to bring those desires to the surface, they are there waiting for us.

I Am Reclaiming My Power

For this meditation practice, I invite you to read the following affirmations out loud. Read them to yourself as you're getting ready for the day to start or end. Look yourself in the mirror as you say them out loud. You have the power to shift your thoughts and identify what you want and need. Starting this practice will remind you that you don't have to wait for someone else to give you the answers you're searching for. You can turn inward and affirm yourself. Take a deep breath in and exhale through an open mouth before reading.

I am reclaiming my power by being honest with myself.

I am reclaiming my power by addressing my pain.

I am reclaiming my power by leaning into vulnerability.

I am reclaiming my power by showing up and not shrinking.

I am reclaiming my power by setting healthy boundaries with myself and others.

I am reclaiming my power by slowing down and identifying my needs.

I am reclaiming my power by tapping into my feelings without shame.

I am reclaiming my power by healing slowly and intentionally.

Meditation

Liberation Through Healing

Dr. Thema Bryant

I work as a trauma psychologist and a professor. I facilitate healing by training and teaching people interested in doing the work of psychology, whether through education, research, advocacy, or activism. My specialty is trauma recovery. And within trauma psychology, I look at the influence of culture on our experiences of trauma and how we heal.

For me, the pathways of healing are found in expressive arts, particularly dance and poetry. I also find deep restoration in individual therapy, community and social support, spirituality, and activism. Those five pathways have been integral for me and my journey. I also integrate those pathways when I'm helping other people heal.

When I was a college student, I was sexually assaulted. I was home in Baltimore, Maryland, on a break when the assault took place. Up until that time, I had always been a good student. I was always on the honor roll or dean's list, and I enjoyed learning. When I returned to campus after the assault, it was hard for me to focus and concentrate. I was depressed and anxious. I had to figure out a way to heal to move forward to a place of wellness.

One of the things I did was go to individual therapy at the university's counseling center. And while I don't currently work at a university counseling center, it is not insignificant that the first position I had after getting my doctorate was as the coordinator of a sexual assault response office at a university. I know what a difference it can make when you have trained, compassionate, and knowledgeable people to help you make sense of your world being upside down.

While in school, I already knew I wanted to be a psychologist, but I am sure a big part of my emphasis on sexual trauma, in particular, was birthed out of my experience. One of the things I discovered is that you often hear survivors tell their stories only when they're in a place of devastation. When I was looking around, I did not see any models of people who had made it to the other side of their pain and found joy. I've found that this is often because people work through their trauma, and then they tuck it away. An essential part of my testimony is when I'm talking to people about my sexual assault. Shattering the silence and shame is critical to our healing work. Talking about my sexual assault from the vantage point of healing and wholeness lets people see and know that we do not have to stay stuck in that place of devastation.

Individual therapy was very helpful, and so was my love for the arts. Many sexual trauma survivors have complicated relationships with their bodies. Some of us are angry with our bodies. Before the assault, I had been a dancer, and I thank my mom for introducing me to the art form growing up. When I was in preschool, she had me at the YMCA in dance classes. Dance gave me a language. It allowed me to tell my story through movement. Before I had the words, I would dance it. That's one of the gifts of creativity—you can say as much or as little as you want to say.

I also write poetry. Like dancing, it gives me a voice and an outlet. I wrote about the assault in my poetry, but many people didn't know what I was talking about. Surprisingly, there were a few people who were tuned in enough to decode what I was saying. They would approach me with empathy and say, "I'm so sorry that happened." The arts gave me permission to heal freely and authentically. It offered me the opportunity to reclaim ownership of myself.

A lot of these experiences are unspeakable, and the shame runs deep. We are told not to talk about it, and that is detrimental to our health and wellness. With my clients, I encourage them to find their voice through writing poetry, especially when it feels hard to talk about it out loud. Trauma makes you feel like you're the only one or that you're different from everyone else. It can often leave people feeling like they're broken and everybody else is fine. I find a deep connection with the gift of community. Being believed and supported changes how we heal. Connecting with people who don't have an identical experience but can relate because of what they've been through is beneficial. It makes folks not feel so isolated. As a practitioner, I find that making space not only for the arts but also for community therapy is essential.

Spirituality also plays a large role in my life and work. Professionally, I've tried to intentionally be a bridge between faith communities and the mental health community. Many times the two are separated. So along with my doctorate in psychology, I have a master's in divinity. I am passionate about helping faith communities give themselves and others permission to tell the truth, and not hide behind scripture. Scripture can be very helpful. And along with scripture, we need to be able to say, "I'm broken, I'm tired, I'm frustrated, I'm mad, I'm depressed," and for that not to be silenced or shameful.

I want to normalize that mental health issues do impact people who love God. People of faith can and do experience trauma, depression, and mental health challenges. There are stories of assault in the Bible. Like many others, I had never heard those stories preached about. But once I learned of them and studied the Word for myself, I discovered other feminist and womanist theologians who have written about these stories from the perspectives of the girls and women who were assaulted. It was healing for me to experience this side of theology and faith.

Eventually, I led a women's ministry for several years, and we openly and freely talked about spirituality, trauma, and mental health. And because I train future psychologists, many have never been educated to ask people about their faith, spirituality, or religion. And for many people, clients and therapists alike, belief is a central part of their meaning-making. Imagine working with someone for months, or even years, and you don't even know how they see the world.

Thinking spirituality and religion are not the therapist's domain doesn't serve our clients. Many times, mental health professionals have either neglected the topic or have said very demeaning and disrespectful things, which makes people not want to come back. We want to avoid that in therapy. We want people to come back. Cultural awareness is about not only race and ethnicity but also people's spirituality and faith. Interestingly enough, probably of no surprise, women, people of color, and people with less education endorse higher spirituality or religiosity. So if our psychological interventions ignore that aspect that is central to the lives of women of color, then as therapists, we are overlooking and underserving them.

Over the years, I've become increasingly attuned with the power of no and the power of honoring my boundaries. It's no surprise that 2020 was a whirlwind year, and as a mental health professional, I was committed to helping and serving my clients and community. Something I learned during that time that pushed me into deeper healing was how and when to say no when it comes to my work life and boundaries. This was very big for me because I want to be available—that's why I got into this work. However, because of the pandemic, life was so overwhelming for all of us.

Finally, so many members of the Black community were seeking services for the first time. While some folks had a slower pace of life in 2020, those in the mental health world were overflowing with trying to help our clients and take care of ourselves and our families. I had to start referring clients to other mental health professionals, and it felt terrible because people were showing up to heal and get help, and I couldn't support them how I wanted. Eventually, I started taking on everyone I could until I couldn't anymore. Life caught up with me, and I realized I needed to press stop and say, "I cannot be everything to everyone," and that was a point of liberation for me during that time. I learned to not only set better boundaries but also honor my humanity and my ability to rest emotionally so that I could show up fully in my work and life. Stillness and solitude are necessary for restoration and healing.

Dr. Thema Bryant *is a psychologist, a minister, an author, and an artist.*

Permission Slips

In this practice, you'll write permission slips for yourself. The idea here is to step away from rigidity and holding yourself hostage to always doing, and instead step into ease, rest, and liberation. Title the top of your page "I Am Allowed To." Create four sections on the same page titled "Heal," "Rest," "Create," and "Find Joy." Fill in each box with things that you're giving yourself permission to do. Do not hold back. No matter how big or small, explore your heart's desires. Explore the things that make you feel seen, safe, and supported. Focus on naming your needs, unfiltered by shame and guilt. In order to reclaim your power, you must allow yourself to take up space, name your needs, and go for what brings you joy.

Journaling

REWRITING YOUR NARRATIVE

Rewriting your story—taking ownership over your narrative and who you want to be—is an essential step in this healing journey. Writing to heal allows us to address the parts of our story that we need to shed in order to move forward with power and confidence. There will be tender moments as we step away from what we once knew and who we once were. That is part of the process. You are in control here. Only you will know when you're ready to put things down on the page. Being prepared to rewrite your narrative will force you to look at the things you've turned away from. This is your story. Do not let fear prevent you from turning over a new leaf. Rewriting your narrative takes bravery, failure, beginning again, and being willing to change.

In my early twenties, I started to make significant changes in my life. I was tired of feeling defeated by my bad choices. My relationships weren't healthy, and I kept trying to fix myself in the same environments that broke me down and left me distracted from doing the healing work I wanted to do. I was lost and unsure how to find my way, but I knew I had to—I knew I wanted to. On my journey to enriching my life, I got a lot of push-back. Some people weren't sure how to cope with the changes I was making and questioned my authenticity. It would've been easier to remain stuck in my old ways, but it would've been detrimental in the long run, making my life much more challenging and less fulfilling. Choosing to rewrite my story, change, and commit to my healing allowed me to grow into my best self. It allowed me to take control of my life and release all the stories I was carrying that didn't belong to me.

Over the years, I've learned the importance of healing my inner child, the practice of being in dialogue with and nurturing my younger self. I was stuck in old ways because of unhealthy learned behaviors from my upbringing. In my youth, I learned to please other people and shrink myself to fit in and be loved. I was constantly searching for external validation to shape me into a lovable person. This meant abandoning my true self and living out a story that I didn't need or want.

As I started making shifts in my life, it became clear that running from my story—the good, the bad, and the heartbreaking—was no longer an option. It hadn't gotten me anywhere. I chose to heal and find comfort in my own company and inner truth. My emotional and spiritual journey reminded me that I was in control of my life. I had the power to grow with or without someone standing next to me. It was a growth spurt that forced me to see myself. I lost friends, family didn't understand me, and I had to figure out how to emotionally support myself alone. Healing while isolated was the scariest part, but I had to outgrow my former self. Having no one but myself, my truth, and my journal wasn't fun, but it encouraged me to finally see myself. Doing this type of soul work alone allowed me to reclaim my power.

Choosing yourself when no one is cheering for you is a revolutionary act. Yes, having people in your corner rooting you on makes you feel good for the moment. But remember, external validation is a bonus, not the goal.

And if you aren't careful it has the power to keep you stuck in a false sense of comfort rather than connected to yourself and your story. External validation isn't what's going to heal you. It's temporary. Healing is solitary work that can be done only by you.

I encourage you to take a step back and look at your life through your own eyes, not through the eyes of your parents, employer, friends, or partner. Who are you? What do you want? How do you wish to rewrite your narrative? It's intimidating to step away from the comfort of others telling us how to be, but healing requires nothing less. See your emotional and mental growth spurts as the nudge you need to look deeper through the eyes of self-commitment, self-exploration, and self-trust.

No one can force you in the direction you need to go in—not a therapist, not a coach, not your favorite author. There are always times when healing must be done by you. After you see a doctor for a broken bone, you don't sit in their office until your bone is healed. You get the care you need and you're sent home to rest and heal on your own time. The same is true when healing on an emotional level. We go home to ourselves, turn inward, and mend one step and day at a time.

As you unpack and rewrite your story, as you tap into your personal truth, you will become familiar with what you know to be true about yourself. Things that you've been hiding from or have a hard time facing will emerge and remind you to lean in. Stay curious about your healing. Turning away will keep you in a loop of shame and regret. Look at the things you need to face and learn from them.

The Craft of Healing
Nneka Julia

At heart, I am an artist and an entrepreneur. I love both the art and science of a lot of things. As a kid, I was always the person scribbling on walls or cutting snowflakes out and pasting them everywhere. There's always just been this external need to create something tangible. I'm so thankful that my parents didn't discourage me even though they believed in following a traditional educational path. And while they weren't going to send me to art school, they embraced my creative spirit and personality.

Eventually, I stopped drawing and painting because I thought I needed to take this linear path toward a career. After college, I worked for the family business for fifteen years until 2021. During that time, I worked with individuals with mental health challenges and developmental disabilities. Being in that line of work and building a business around the care of others has shaped how I view business and relationships. It's taught me so much about compassion and community as an extension of myself.

When you experience changing an adult's diaper or giving medication to someone, and you've dealt with individuals who are very unseen and invisible to most of society, you hone the skill of making people feel seen and safe. Not only that, but you also learn how to self-reflect on a deeper level. I often left work asking myself what makes me feel seen.

I've always loved photographs. Looking through my father's albums is something I enjoy doing. He and my mom have done a great job documenting their lives. When I was twenty, I discovered this big bucket of photos that I'd never seen before. And I was like, *Man, I don't think I've done a good enough job of capturing people and things the way my parents have.* I'd done a great job putting stuff on Facebook, but I wanted to do more of what my parents had done—capturing moments and experiences that would otherwise be lost. This led me to take my dad's camera for a little bit. He made it clear that I couldn't have it, and he wanted it back. So I saved some money, bought a Nikon, and started taking photos.

As the middle child, I didn't like being the center of attention. When I picked up photography, I learned that the craft showed the beauty of being seen by the way I saw and captured what was around me. When people look at a photograph, they are looking at the world through your eyes. That was and still is astonishing to me.

I started traveling and collecting these visual stories. Going into places and meeting people, I realized that Instagram and social media are very one-dimensional.

I would be riding on the back of a camel and going through a breakup, and everybody would just see the camel. As much as I loved making images and sharing them, it became a very shallow way to communicate. I never viewed photos like that. They've always held such depth to me. However, when the sharing is simplified to a square through your phone, the images are often viewed solely as aesthetically pleasing or aspirational. Nobody knows what is going on in your life. I started to ask myself, *What lessons am I imparting? What am I* really *leaving behind if it's just beauty?*

When I started my podcast, that's when I took writing a bit more seriously. I'd always been writing, jotting down, keeping journals, and things like that, but never to the point of wanting to share the stories. Deciding to share my stories was a turning point. Marrying images with words and audio created a deep sense of connection to my work and the world around me. There were times where I felt so alone writing and recording the stories. But then someone from across the globe would reach out, sharing how much they could relate. There's comfort in knowing that I'm not the only one who has been hurt. I think sharing that part of myself is vital. Written story-telling has changed my life and is the nucleus of how I've healed and continue to heal.

The breakup that I went through was tough. It left me trying to make sense of the pain I was feeling. My appetite vanished. I was sleeping all day and had sunk into what I now see was a deep depression. Writing about it now and being in a completely different emotional space is challenging. But as an artist, I know that my experiences and stories aren't in vain. Someone out there may be able to relate and take some nuggets of wisdom from what I walked through.

My journey to more profound healing was kick-started when I realized that none of my answers was external. Dealing with heartbreak was proof that absolutely no one was going to save me. No guru was going to come down and tell me that everything was going to be okay. Nothing could magically make my ex love me or make me love myself responsibly. It had to come from me.

I am my center place—a place I can always return to. Over the years, I've come to know that everyone will be okay. Living through 2020 was proof that stepping away to take care of myself and heal when I needed it wouldn't hurt anyone. Everybody will live if you remove yourself for a little bit. It's okay to make yourself a priority.

As I hone my craft and continue creating and capturing stories, I often ask myself, *How am I leaving people better than how they were before?* Healing has taught me to be in flow. When I find that place, time and space vanish. Photography and writing serve as an invitation to slow down and be more intentional. Storytelling, from oration to the written word, is how I heal. I am a collector of stories.

Nneka Julia *is a writer, photographer, and podcast host.*

What Is My Story?

This writing practice is centered around your story so that you can reclaim what belongs to you and release what doesn't. Use the list of questions below to begin to connect with your authentic story, the story that reflects your values, dreams, and joy. Do not do these questions all at once. Pace yourself and take time to sit with each question.

What stories do not belong to me that I'm holding on to?

How do I want to start this new chapter of my life?

What stories, good or bad, have shaped me?

What would I want a book about my legacy to say?

What do I need to stop talking myself out of?

Are there any stories I need to release or to stop replaying?

Journaling

MAKING PEACE WITH OLD STORIES

If you don't forgive yourself or let go of old narratives, healing will be hard to come by. Holding yourself hostage and hating yourself for your past mistakes will not support your longing to heal or create the ease in your life that you want. I spent years in the depth of my pain because I thought I deserved it. A lot of my trauma and emotional distress came from my childhood. I felt that self-hatred was normal. Self-love and forgiveness of myself and others were foreign to me.

There was no one in my life teaching me how to love myself. I lacked the tools to claim my personal power and had to figure out how to show up for myself on my own. I often joke that I failed my way through self-forgiveness. Now I see the many failures as a blessing in disguise, but back then I was angry and confused. When toxicity and inner turmoil feel like the standard, change feels otherworldly. It took years of therapy, self-reflection, failing, and processing on my journal pages to undo that mindset. Unlearning the dysfunctional things I'd been carrying so close to my heart for such a long time was a huge mountain to climb.

In childhood, I wanted the attention of my mostly absent father; in adulthood, I vied for the attention of emotionally absent men and friends. All of this dug me deeper into self-destruction. At that point in my life, I figured I would live that way until the day I died. I harmed myself for years before I decided it was time to turn the tables and start over. Emotional self-harm was a beast to unlearn and it created even more to do when I finally started to scratch the surface of my healing.

As I was healing, I realized that I chose to stay down and out as a punishment. I thought it would teach me a lesson. Most of my suffering was self-inflicted because I lacked self-worth. I didn't believe my life was worth anything. And because of that defeating way of thinking, joy and healing didn't feel within my reach. I ended up reinforcing the lie that I couldn't trust myself or my thoughts. With that leading my life, I tried to fill my heart with external validation and unhealthy, codependent relationships.

When we hate and mistreat ourselves, for whatever reason, we stunt our emotional growth and we hush empathy and self-compassion. We lose ourselves and our hope in the pain. The ability to create a new path seems to get further and further away. Many of us have done and said things—and acted in ways that we regret—because of the emotional and mental state we were in. We cannot take back our missteps or bad behavior. We cannot make things vanish. And, even in our errors, failures, and challenges, we do not deserve the further distress we inflict on ourselves for something we cannot change. What we *do* have the power to change is our outlook. Offering love to the parts of ourselves we've hated for so long takes dedication and practice.

We deserve to show up in this work flawed. Getting it right all the time is impossible. There is no arrival point in healing. As long as we are alive, we will continue to grow, fail, succeed, and learn along the way. After many years of doing my own deep healing work, I've come to know that our answers are buried within us. We all hold the power to reclaim our truth and share our true beauty and joy with the world.

It's easy to talk ourselves out of doing the work we need to change. But becoming who we wish to become in this life requires acknowledging and releasing who we used to be. It calls us to recognize our patterns and put action behind changing them. We can get wrapped up in our minds about how we should be showing up and healing. We can feel isolated because people around us refuse to understand or do their own soul work.

Remember what your work is. Inner peace starts when you stop trying to change people who do not want to change. Your healing and their healing are not synonymous. Making peace with yourself and your past looks like pushing through and breaking cycles of dysfunction, trauma, and self-hatred. When you choose to heal yourself, you actively choose to heal the generations after you.

Let this work show you what it's like to lean into grace. We are in constant ebb and flow when it comes to learning self-love, inner peace, and deepening our connection with who we are striving to be. We cannot hate ourselves into being better versions of ourselves. It's impossible. Love, patience, and understanding have to be at the center of our healing.

A writing practice serves as the invitation to put things down, literally, so that you can embrace a new story. Many of us have been holding on to old versions of ourselves because we don't know where to put them. Our emotional suitcases are so full that there's no room for change because there's no space. Abandoning yourself isn't working. This practice of healing and evolving requires you to be fully present and committed. Standing in your power looks like not settling or quitting when life gets hard. Reclaiming your voice means freeing yourself from the confines of the box you've been living in for far too long. You have the power to tell a new story.

Healing in Slowing Down
Chriselle Lim

Alex Elle: Who are you and what do you do?

Chriselle Lim: First and foremost, I am a mother to two girls. I have a seven-year-old and a three-year-old, and I am a digital entrepreneur. I started my career as a content creator. Some people know me from my YouTube channel. Some people know me from TikTok as Rich Mom. Some people know me from my fashion sense on Instagram. I also have a company called Bümo. It's all about the future of family and figuring out solutions for modern, working, millennial parents.

AE: How has healing shown up in your life?

CL: Healing has shown up during a tough time for me. Going through my divorce brought a lot of things to the surface. A lot of my healing process requires waiting and being still. That was the hardest part for me. The most challenging part of healing is sitting with ourselves, our souls, and just observing ourselves without judgment or harsh critique. I live a fast-paced life, and going through a divorce forced me to slow everything down and get to know myself better. We all get so busy with our lives, and sometimes we want to get through things just to get through them and have it done with—but I knew that I couldn't do it with divorce. I had to grieve properly and make space for myself. I'm still healing today, but I think I am doing it in a very healthy way.

AE: What did going through a divorce teach you about yourself?

CL: A lot! But the main thing is that when you're married and have kids, you let a lot of things slide just to make sure that the family is comfortable. I ended up being at the bottom of my priority list until I broke. I've been talking to other women lately—divorced, married, and single women—and the stories are all similar. We all seem to be conditioned to put other people before ourselves. This is something that I would like to change, especially when it comes to mothers. Growing up with immigrant parents, I often heard that they had to sacrifice everything to make sure the family and kids were happy, safe, and in one unit. As women, we turn a blind eye to many things, including our pain, wants, and needs, because of that. We push away our fears, problems, triggers, and things that bother us to keep the family unit intact, and I want to destigmatize women *not* doing that. We don't have to settle or be last on our list.

AE: What creative modalities have you used to heal?

CL: Because I've been so tied to my work and family, there was no breathing room for me to explore what I enjoyed outside of those two things. I'm still figuring out what it is that brings me so much joy outside of work and kids. Two things that I do find myself doing a lot more are reading and traveling. Because I am co-parenting, I have more time to enjoy those two things. That has been healing for me. Before, I never traveled for myself or to explore and see new things. I was always on the road for work. It would be in and out. I didn't get to enjoy the places I went to. And so now my absolute favorite thing to do is get through a book. I like being able to hop on a long flight somewhere, finish the book, get off the flight, and just explore. I feel very grateful that I have the ability, time, and finances to do that. Having more time to get to know me and what I like has been inspiring. I look forward to exploring other things, like sports or art. I am open.

AE: How does taking a break from healing help you replenish yourself?

CL: I believe in therapy, self-improvement, and aiming to become a better person. I love learning more about myself and growing into the best version of myself. Sometimes that hinders me from being in the moment, living freely, and actually applying what I've learned in life. The first six months of my divorce, I was so obsessed with making sure I was constantly reading a book or listening to a helpful podcast. I was in a constant state of trying to heal and be my best. But over time, that changed, and my emotional rest now looks like reading fiction books. For me, that is so bizarre because I hated fiction. I thought it was pointless and useless because I wanted the things that would help me improve my life. I've learned that I can trust myself. I have the tools to heal, and I don't have to be obsessed with them or constantly improve myself. Emotional rest for me also looks like listening to music without feeling guilty that I'm not being "productive." Giving myself permission to walk or drive around with nowhere to go feels so refreshing. I don't always have to go somewhere or do something. I can just be. Emotional rest is believing that I can tap into my tools and emotions when needed, but I can also be creative and live in a fantasy world of fiction books when I want to and not feel bad about it—that heals me too.

AE: How do you heal?

CL: I heal by giving myself grace and compassion, accepting my flaws, and knowing that I'm still a work in progress. I heal by hanging out with my girlfriends as much as possible, surrounding myself with people who get me and don't judge me. I heal by connecting with people and sharing stories and being vulnerable. I heal by having an open heart, knowing that anything is possible now.

Chriselle Lim *is a fashion stylist, lifestyle and beauty blogger, and digital entrepreneur.*

Walk It Out

Walking has become a big part of my healing journey. I love being under the open sky and feeling the earth beneath my feet as I turn a question over in my mind. During this walking meditation, consider the following: "What stories do not belong to me that I'm holding on to?" Start your sentence off with "The stories that don't belong to me are . . . " and list the things that speak to you. Ask yourself where you learned this and how it makes you feel today. Hold space for anything that comes up.

Give yourself time to process what comes up and be patient with yourself as you turn inward. Remember, you know how to find your answers. You have what it takes to identify the ways you want to change, shift, and grow. Be patient and compassionate with yourself as you listen to yourself rewriting your story and changing your narrative.

Meditation

NURTURING YOUR INNER CHILD

Learning to hold space for our inner child or younger self can feel like an odd concept. We're grown now. Why do we need to go back and unearth our deep pain or trauma?

I had that same question, and it wasn't until I started exploring the deep grief that seemed to come out of nowhere in my adult life that I realized almost all of my pain was related to things that happened in my formative younger years. There were things I'd never shared in therapy and pushed away because I thought they were not relevant. But *of course* feeling rejected by my father and hated by my mother would impact me in real and painful ways for the duration of my life.

When I started writing my book *After the Rain*, I realized just how brokenhearted I was about my childhood. Writing that book felt like an unearthing of suffering— but it was also liberating. During that process, I wrote letters to my younger self, hoping that would soothe some of the wounds I'd reopened. I've carried the loneliness and hurt of my childhood so close that it was hard to let myself feel safe. I also realized just how much of my trauma was generational and unhelpful to the emotional healing I was trying to do. Coming to this recollection at thirty years old made me frustrated. I'd done all this work, and the pain I was walking through did not reflect the emotional strides I had made.

I avoided inner-child work because I was terrified about what would come up, but I knew I had to get to the bottom of this newly emerged sadness. Nurturing our inner child helps us identify what is ours, emotionally, and what is not. We're often conditioned to carry the pain and projections of others, almost like these things belong to us. We often get confused when it comes to healing because we aren't clear about what is ours to tend to and what is not. Showing up for ourselves on the page allows us the space to sort through things that may or may not belong in our emotional suitcases.

I eased my way into this practice by writing letters to the little girl in me and offering her the comfort, love, and care I wished I'd been given. I told her things like "You're safe now," "I love you," and "The trauma wasn't your fault." I gave myself room and grace to fall apart. Nurturing my younger self on the page welcomed me and all my messiness. It demanded me to offer respect, compassion, and solace to myself. I learned to comfort the child in me because she needed and deserved my attention.

This work may feel difficult or strange to you, and I encourage you to welcome that discomfort. I tell my students who do this deep introspective work that our inner child *is* us. There's no separating our current self from our younger self. The experiences we had growing up, good and bad, can and will impact us. Ignoring our experiences is neglecting ourselves. We must learn to live in tandem with both and offer consideration to the broken parts of ourselves. That is how we make peace with ourselves and step intentionally into our healing. It's how we learn to find harmony and acceptance. It's where we learn how to love ourselves and flourish in our healing.

Trying to be perfect will distract you from digging deep and getting your hands dirty. Leave perfection at the door. This is messy work. When you show up on the page with flaws and vulnerability in tow, you will discover so much about yourself and your resilience. Your pain can be a pathway to growth. Inner-child work is the place for that. It's where you can break and heal as much as you need to without judgment, shame, or guilt. No matter your circumstances, your inner child needs your attention. You can empower yourself on the page and find new ways to be your own greatest teacher and ally.

As you work through these practices, remember that your inner child is part of your story. Welcome them, engage with them. Do not silence them. Let them help you grow in your power. Their voice is your voice.

Inner-Child Reflection

Our inner child is our original or true self. It's also the hidden childlike part of our personality characterized by playfulness, spontaneity, and creativity. When our inner child gets triggered, it can lead to anger, hurt, and fear that we don't understand or that seems outsized compared to the actual trigger. These journal prompts invite you to get curious about what your wants and needs looked like as a child and what they look like now.

What does your inner child need today?
What made you feel safe and loved as a child?
What made you feel fearful and silenced growing up?

Were you creative as a child? If so, how?
What did you like to create?

What would you change about your childhood?
What would you keep the same?

Journaling

Inner-Child Affirmation

Read this meditation out loud into the voice memo app on your device. Create a ritual out of listening to the playback. Perhaps you make your favorite tea, cook a nice meal for yourself, or run a warm bath to prepare for some intentional time. Allow this practice to be your moment of self-love reflection and inner peace. Set a reminder to replay this inner-child affirmation as often as you need.

Dear younger self,

You are safe. I am creating a good life for you. Even on the days I am lost, I trust that a new direction or path will emerge. I love you deeply. I'm sorry for ever making you feel like I didn't. I was learning then and I am learning now. I am dedicated to my healing because of you. What you didn't have then, you have now. Thank you for reminding me that I can show up for myself. Thank you for not giving up on me. You've shown me that I can be who I've always wanted to be. You are safe. You are loved. I am here.

Meditation

Rock-and-Roll Breathing

Being deep in our healing means feeling everything that rises and falls. This breathwork exercise is perfect for getting you out of your head and into your body. It's a grounding breath that encourages you to connect deeper to release feelings of stagnation.

Sit in a comfortable position, on the floor or a cushion with your back supported.

Place your hands on your belly as you inhale.

While inhaling, lean forward and expand your belly.

On your exhale, squeeze the breath out, curving your spine while leaning backward, emptying your belly.

Repeat this breathing pattern six times. Do it slowly and intentionally. While breathing, envision yourself in a place of peace, calm, and ease. Even if things feel rocky in your life today, you can always come back to your breath.

Breathwork

LESSONS AND LETTERS TO YOUR YOUNGER SELF

To stand in your power, you have to practice speaking about yourself with positivity and confidence. But learning to use positive, self-affirming language can be really challenging for many of us. I was so accustomed to speaking negatively to myself that practicing doing the opposite felt counterintuitive. Even with the challenges I faced along the way, I knew the only path home to myself was one that required me to intentionally choose not to keep belittling and blaming myself. I found it extremely challenging at first to speak kindly to my adult self, the self that I scolded for not knowing better or doing better. What helped me get to a place of grace and self-compassion over the years was the practice of writing letters to my younger self—being her mentor, if you will.

This inner-child work changed me. It not only showed me the possibility of having a loving relationship with myself, but it allowed me to self-soothe in new ways. It pushed me to talk to myself like someone I cared for and loved. Being compassionate about everything that came up on the page from childhood—the good and the bad—encouraged me to be gentle toward myself. Slowing down to care for and listen to myself felt like a new language I had to learn.

I learned on this path of growing, forgiving, and loving myself that when we commit to emotional restoration, we commit to seeing ourselves without judgment. Hating ourselves doesn't help us heal; it stunts our growth and keeps us small. Comforting our inner child, forgiving our shortcomings, releasing the habit of self-blame, and choosing to begin again can bring a newfound sense of identity and beauty in life.

We are made for this work, this life, and this self-love. What we lacked emotionally and tangibly growing up doesn't mean we didn't deserve it or that we were worthy of the suffering we endured. We cannot keep lying to ourselves and hiding from the things that break our hearts. When I stopped blaming myself for what I did or didn't do, I started becoming more open to the possibility of true expansion and self-nurturing. I often remind my younger self to go into her dark places, bring it all to light, and refuse to suffer in silence.

We can reparent ourselves by listening to our past and present needs. This process is life-changing. Growing up, I didn't have people listening—like listening with their whole body and with a sense of understanding and care. So as I reparent myself, I'm learning to listen to my needs and my desires, both from today and from my younger years. We can make up for what we lacked in childhood by showing up for ourselves now. We can shift how we look at our past and marvel at how we've evolved and what we've learned along the way. We get to decide how we learn and grow now, as adults.

Healing in Therapy
Luvvie Ajayi Jones

I'm a multi-hyphenate. I'm an author, a speaker, and a podcast host. But no matter the *how*, I'm passionate about creating work that helps people feel joy and think critically, and compels them to take action that leaves this world better than they found it.

Healing showed up in my life more than five years ago in therapy, and the catalyst for it was experiencing backlash online. It knocked me on my ass, and I realized I didn't have the tool kit I needed to deal with being a visible person whose words can be weaponized.

It is already hard enough to be a Black woman. Being a visible Black woman means I'm constantly dealing with people's projections of who they think I am, and I'm dealing with it in the harshest of ways. I was already going through my own shit, and then I had to figure out how to navigate outside projections and other people's shit. It was overwhelming, so I sought out therapy.

I knew therapy was necessary when I realized that I needed to be even more steadfast about my worth and more focused on who I am, not other people's ideas of who I might be. Of course, going to therapy unfolded all types of things, and it became apparent that there was a lot of trauma I'd been carrying and not dealing with or acknowledging. Therapy pulled one thread, and suddenly it seemed like my whole sweater came undone. I thought I was there for one thing, and it quickly became evident that I was there for many things.

My healing work was multifaceted, and my first therapist, Dr. Patterson, was a healing and grounding presence for me. She died suddenly in 2021 and that rocked me! I learned about her passing a day before meeting with her for our next session, and that loss in itself peeled back another layer of healing and grief that I had to process. Who I am today is a testament to our work together, which is why she's all up through my second book, *Professional Troublemaker*. Dr. P was able to help me unlock vulnerability, and she helped me start dealing with repressed trauma. We don't often realize how much of our life is traumatic because identifying it as that is in itself being vulnerable.

One of the many tools Dr. P gave me is actively learning and practicing not to run away from the hard stuff, something no one had previously taught me. I hadn't encountered that way of thinking. Until working with her and starting to deal with my experiences head-on, I didn't realize that I had spent a lot of my life running away from facing the hard stuff. We busy ourselves with life, work, and even playing on our phones. Dr. P was the first person who told me to stop running so fast.

In working with Dr. P, I found a deeper understanding of healing as a spectrum. I don't think we're ever done healing. We are constantly unlearning the habits that we picked up from others. We learn along the way to put down other people's projections about us, and we ultimately discover how to become stronger and softer people because of it.

Dr. P's death stunned me. Who helps you process the sudden death of the person who helps you process life? I found out she died in the middle of a hectic workday. I forced myself to compartmentalize the news until my day was over. I put the fact into a little box and put that box away in a tiny corner of my chest. My workday didn't end until 8 p.m. that day. By 8:05, I was sobbing.

As a writer, I process everything through words, so I wrote about her and how she transformed my life. Her impact on my healing was profound and grounding. As I was writing about her death, I found myself hearing her voice and what she would say to me as if she were walking me through her own death. This is what I imagined:

Dr. P: *So how are you feeling today?*

Me: *I guess I'm okay.*

Dr. P, silent and looking at me intently.

Me: *I'm not okay. Your death has thrown me for a major loop. I don't know how to handle it, so I'm just working and writing through it.*

Dr. P: *What are you avoiding by working through it?*

Me: *The realization that I'm feeling a loss that feels really big and really personal, and I'm feeling selfish about it because I don't know if I'm mourning you or mourning what you not being here means for me.*

Dr. P: *Is there a difference?*

Me: *I don't know.*

It felt like even in her death, she was teaching me how to tap into myself and be honest with my feelings. That is a testament to her amazing work and ability to help people heal, see, and feel. In spirit, she was right there and I was processing with her. As she taught me, I sat with and in what I'd learned rather than running away from it. Having my therapist, the person helping me process life, die was an invitation to actively use the tools she'd given me. I saw at that moment how much I'd learned and grown.

I have a new therapist now who encourages me to write things down. She knows that I haven't processed whatever I've been going through if I don't write. There are times when I go for months without journaling because I'm not ready to face hard things.

I think it's important to give myself room to emotionally rest and be a mess sometimes. That feels necessary for my healing. It takes a little bit of the pressure off and reminds me that I don't always have to get it right. Choosing to take time to rest reminds me that even when I'm not doing the work, I am still valuable and worthy. When you do a lot of hard work or healing, you need to take a break afterward. Just like athletes take a break—emotional rest is like the off-season. I don't have to constantly work to be better every second. There are days when I need to just be a mess, and that's okay.

I heal by going to therapy.

I heal by surrounding myself with people who fill my spirit with joy.

I heal by trying as much as possible to be gentle with myself because I can be very self-critical.

I heal by staying in my integrity.

Luvvie Ajayi Jones *is an author, a speaker, and a podcaster.*

Journaling

Listen to Your Inner Child

To better understand the story that brought us to this moment, we must acknowledge the wants and needs of our inner child. Those wants and needs shaped the person we are today. In this practice, you'll be identifying your inner child's desires and needs on the pages of your journal. I invite you to think about what you wanted and needed emotionally in childhood that you felt you did not get.

Title the top of a blank journal page "My Younger Self." Draw a T-chart underneath, then label one side "Wanted" and the other side "Needed." Start a list, alternating between each side, writing down the first words (not phrases) that come to mind. This is key to drawing your attention to one thing to unpack later.

Now that you have lists of words for what you "Wanted" and "Needed," set a timer for two minutes and allow yourself to freewrite in each of the columns. To freewrite, keep your pen on the page and do not pause to overthink or fix anything. Try to fill in as much of the chart as you can within the two minutes. You may have short lists or very long ones; there is no right or wrong way to do this practice.

MAKING PEACE WITH YOUR PAST

As we look back on our stories, there will be reminders of where we fell short or completely messed up. Each of us has something we aren't proud of or would rather not remember. Examining our past can feel daunting because there is no escaping that we have gotten things wrong, hurt someone's feelings, or backtracked to old bad habits that we know don't serve us. Some of us find it incredibly painful to look at our past because we may have been victimized and just want the shame and pain to vanish.

Discomfort isn't something any of us *want* to feel. It's a nod to the challenges we've had to endure and what it means to have lived through something, even if that something changed us or hurt us in the worst way. It's complicated to face what is still tender. We want to heal, but we don't know where or how to start. Making peace with our past requires us to look at everything that has broken us down and shaken us up, even if it makes us cringe.

We are worthy of comfort and ease even if we have a painful past. Refusing to look at the history that shapes us hinders us from doing the deep healing. When we begin to dismantle the control our past has over our life, we begin to make peace with ourselves. Our past is not our enemy; it is our teacher. Be open to the guidance it can offer.

I invite you to be curious about the fears and pain points of your past. Look them in the eye and see what they're trying to say. Give yourself permission to greet each lesson with as little judgment as possible, and be lenient with the process of sorting through it all. You deserve the same flexibility and grace in your healing that you offer others. If a loved one were struggling with the hurt of their past, what would you say? How would you support them? How would you love and show up for them? How would you listen and hold space? Now be that to yourself. You are here in this life to learn and expand.

When we make peace with the past, we open the door to emotional safety and self-trust, allowing us to delve even deeper. In time, you can even stop punishing yourself for your past. To be with your tender heart is to be with your whole self.

Cultivate Self-Belief

As we reclaim our power, we are rebuilding our self-belief—
what we know to be good and true about ourselves.
Intentional breathing can help us usher out the shame, guilt,
and doubt and replace it with strength, peace, and love. As
you reflect on your self-belief and make room for peace,
practice this breathing technique.

Your inhale should be long and slow. As you exhale, pretend
that you're blowing into a bubble wand, long and slow.
Repeat this four times with your eyes closed and your body
soft. You can do this sitting, lying down, or walking.

Inhale self-belief (long and slow).

Exhale shame (long and slow).

Inhale inner peace (long and slow).

Exhale guilt (long and slow).

Inhale self-love (long and slow).

Exhale self-doubt (long and slow).

Breathwork

Healing Your Heart

As we do this deep, healing work, we can begin to come up for air and see the world around us more clearly. We are all dealing with unspoken and unseen things, some heavier to carry than others. If writing and healing have taught me anything, it's that being human is a hard job, and all we can do is our best. We will face experiences that will stay with us—hurt us and heal us. Our hearts will break, grief will strike, but with the right tools, we can find the courage to brave the storms and keep living with grace and joy.

Resilience is in our blood, even when it feels like we are at the weakest point. Something that stays with me most is that I don't always have to be okay. Keeping this idea close reminds me to see the humanity and healing in others. Everyone's path to sorting through turbulent emotions, big feelings, and deep pain is monumentally different.

Years ago, I lived in an apartment building with a woman who never looked happy. She wasn't the least bit pleasant in passing. She was known as The Mean Lady. Ms. Paula, who sat at the front desk, used to mumble about her under her breath. I'd smile and speak to her every time I saw her. I was probably the most annoying person in her eyes, but I didn't care. She would look at me with a blank expression and rarely returned a hello; if she did speak, it was under her breath and clearly out of obligation. Her face was often plastered with an angry look. She looked hurt and overwhelmed. Her daughter, who was seven or eight, always exuded the opposite energy and clung to her mother. It was almost like she was tasked with protecting her mother from something or someone.

I often wondered what The Mean Lady was going through, how she was feeling, and what was aching her. Having that repeated experience with my neighbor made me realize that we never know what people are going through. Every scoff, every eye roll, and every sucking of the teeth I felt viscerally. My heart broke for her.

"Stop speaking to that lady," my husband would say. I'd laugh and say, "Nope, she's going to speak back one day." Secretly, I deeply related and empathized with her because I knew the feeling of wearing my pain on my face, of feeling so angry that I'd want to burn down buildings. I'd felt so let down by life that I'd wanted to scream, "Screw you and your joy and your perfect life!" to every passerby who dared to look at me.

Sometimes, I'd see her coming toward the elevator, and she'd be hesitant to get in. I figured she was thinking, "There's that chatty lady from the third floor again." But I'd hold the door anyway. She'd reluctantly get in. Eventually, I stopped saying hello and just smiled at her.

I figured I could be warm without selfishly trying to force her to speak to me.

One day, I smiled at her, and she smiled back. I almost fell over from surprise. It'd been months and months of silence and pained looks. Now I wondered what had shifted, what had softened in her. What had happened that made her smile back at me? I was so happy for this stranger, and I oddly felt a sense of sisterhood. Pushing my luck a bit further, I said, "Nice day, huh?" It was beautiful outside. Not too warm yet, and breezy. Fluffy white clouds floating by. Spring flowers starting to make their appearance. I was in an exceptionally good mood that day, and it was nice to see her in a good mood, too. She replied, "Yeah, today's a good one," nodding in my direction and making eye contact. "Yeah, it is," I said, beaming. I walked into my unit and said to my husband, "The Mean Lady spoke to me!" I was ecstatic. "And I don't think she's mean per se—but I do think she's hurting."

I became more curious about her after that, wondering if she'd been divorced or widowed. Did she have to leave her home in another state to come here? What had she witnessed that broke her? How was she repairing her life and starting over? In my husband's words, I was being nosy, but I genuinely felt curious. I wanted to know her story, but I didn't dare ask or cross that boundary. I continued to see her and smile. We never spoke again after that, but she was warm to me. More open. Less like I was on her nerves and more like we had an unspoken understanding of "I see you" and "thank you."

We eventually moved from the building, and I've wondered many times over the years how she and her daughter are doing. Whenever they come to mind, I say a little prayer and send a little smile. I chuckle when I think about her annoyance for me. And I wonder if she tells stories about me, the lady who always wanted to say hi and smile. My hope is that she felt, even for an instant, connected and aware that we are never alone in this life, even when we feel defeated at every turn.

I share this story because compassion and connection are central to all the work we are doing here. As you commit to the work of healing your heart, you will begin to see outside your own experience and see that we are all shouldering our share of pain. It's interesting to witness the healing of a heart—the lightening of a spirit—even when it's from a distance and even when we don't know the person intimately. In bearing witness to the hurt and healing of others, we can see our own healing on a deeper and more intentional level. I'm reminded of the beauty that can present itself when we choose to be a mirror as we walk in the world. We miss so much if we are not in tune or intentional with how we're moving, living, and seeing our surroundings. We miss opportunities to connect with, love, and smile at the stranger in the elevator who may need it. We miss our moment to be introspective and gracious to ourselves for making it as far as we've come.

I could have easily been nasty to my neighbor. The old, unhealed me would have likely returned the hostility. But that would have done nothing for either of us. What she needed was kindness, calm, and someone to see her. I know that to be true because I'd been there. I'd been so hardened and hurt at one point in my life that I just wanted someone to see me and smile with their eyes and say with their body language that I wasn't alone, and the load would lighten.

Feeling alone is hard. Being alone is hard. And thinking "life won't get better" is compounded by the two.

Healing our hearts is so much more than a solitary act. It is communal. As we heal, we give others the permission to do the same. Leading by example, especially after you've walked through your storms, is such a gift to the world around us. It's a nod to those bearing witness to us that the light will shine again, and if life feels heavy to hold today, it won't be dark or lonely forever.

Slow Healing

Barb Schmidt

I am a seeker of truth. I teach people how to come into their own by coming home to themselves. As a mindfulness and meditation practitioner, I'm here to help people see that their relationship with themselves is what matters most in their lives, which will be the foundation of everything they do.

Growing up, my life was a mess. My parents were both alcoholics and fought constantly. We had very little money. I was the oldest of five children, and I felt like I was the least favorite. I felt early on in my life that I had to be an adult right off the bat—so I never felt like I was a child.

I grew up feeling isolated. No one was allowed over to our home except family, and I had no friends at school. When my mom was drinking, I never knew what would be waiting for me when I came home after school. In my mind, everyone else at school had a perfect life, so I felt like

I had to keep my family a secret. I never wanted anyone to see what kind of life I was living as a young person.

The one thing that anchored me was my Catholic faith. I thought that if I did everything right, God would approve of me. But when I was thirteen, my life changed. My adult uncle came to live with us, and he sexually abused me.

We had no money growing up, so we ate at fast-food restaurants a lot. I remember we went to McDonald's because, back then, they would give you a free hamburger or a cheeseburger for every A that you got on your report card. I was constantly striving to get all As. On one visit, a sign on the door read "Help wanted." I applied—I was fourteen years old. They hired me, and it changed my life. I ended up working five jobs at one point—as a hair washer in a hair salon, as a McDonald's employee, delivering newspapers, working at a dress shop, and cleaning my Spanish teacher's house. Anything to get me out of the house, making money, and away from the abuse is what I did. I remember thinking that there were two parts of me: a person who was thriving and a person who was suffering and traumatized.

The only way I could keep going was to pretend it wasn't happening. If I stopped or slowed down, the feelings became overwhelming. I focused completely on work and tried to block out the shame and self-disgust. I wanted to always be at work. If I could be at work as much as possible, then everything would be okay. It was as if I had two separate lives, and I pretended my home life wasn't real.

Despite my trauma and pain, I was the best employee. Everyone loved me at McDonald's, and I loved them. At work, everything was fantastic. I was making money and handing it over to my parents to make ends meet. I figured this would be my path to success: being the best at my job and making sure that people liked me.

My life changed when I was sixteen and the McDonald's store promoted me to manager. With my new salary, I finally had enough money to move out. I graduated high school early and moved into my own apartment. I worked seven days a week, as many hours as I could. For a while I thought I was doing okay because of the recognition I got for being a good employee. I measured my success by how much the people around me liked me. It didn't even cross my mind to think about how much I didn't like myself.

In the late 1970s, if you earned and saved enough money as a McDonald's employee, the McDonald's Corporation would fund three-year ownership of a store. I ended up owning my own restaurant at twenty-two years old. I was one of the first women out there to get this opportunity. It was my fast track to deeper people-pleasing tendencies. Everything that happened to me on the inside, compounded by the trauma, got transferred into being everything that I could possibly be in the outside world—because that's what mattered most.

When I was twenty-two years old, one day a supervisor came in to bring me an award. He said, "Barbara, we're so happy with your work. We love everything that you're doing. Personally, I can tell that you really love what you're doing because you've put on weight since I've met you."

The last phrase was all I heard. I didn't hear anything else. The comment about my weight devasted me. I left the award at the store. I don't even know what happened to it. In my mind, his words were: *You're not good enough because you're fat.*

I developed the eating disorder bulimia. I suffered from bulimia for about six years, until I could no longer face it on my own. One morning, I woke up and couldn't get out of bed. I remember saying to myself, *I'm not going to work.* I had never missed a day of work or called in sick. A voice in my head said, *Barbara, if you don't get help, you're going to die.*

The trauma and pain I'd boxed away were bursting at the seams. I couldn't hide them anymore. I knew I needed help. I opened the newspaper, and it had a story about how Karen Carpenter had died the year before from anorexia, and on the reverse of that page was an advertisement for a treatment center in Naples, Florida.

I called and asked if I could check myself in. I mustered the strength and drove to Naples and checked myself into treatment. Immediately I thought I had made a terrible mistake. I was put into a single room with just a bed—no TV, no phone, no distractions. They said you couldn't call home for six weeks. I was there, alone, for eight weeks. My first night there I cried. I was scared, but for the first time I also felt free. At the treatment center I was completely cut off from the news and everything happening in the world. I left my life behind. It was a relief to have this respite from constantly trying to keep up with what everyone else thought I should be, look, and act like. This is when my healing started.

I started to unpack the emotional suffering, abuse, trauma, and disconnection from myself in therapy. Joyce, my therapist, saved my life. She encouraged me to open up and talk about my emotions. In my time with her, I realized that I was so numb that I couldn't feel. Reflecting was complicated and challenging. I had no emotions to access for a long time. Talking to Joyce, I started to unwind all the fears and anxieties that I had been carrying for more than half my life. Before that I had been living completely in my own head.

Joyce told me that what happened with my uncle wasn't my fault. She asked me if I wanted to confront my uncle about what had happened or if I wanted to tell my parents. I said no, and she immediately honored my choice, and said, "I can feel that you are getting what you need, and there are ways you can continue, without telling them. I can see this would not be in your best interest or theirs."

Treatment included yoga, group therapy, mindful eating, meditation, and regular exercise. An important part of my healing process was finding a community of people where I felt like I belonged. After eight weeks, I left the treatment center, and I continued to go to AA meetings and support groups. I found ways to incorporate yoga, therapy, meditation, and exercise into my daily routine.

The last thing I wanted to do was to go back to the person I was, so I did all of it. I had a sponsor to whom I talked every day, and I was passionate about staying in recovery. Healing was a slow process that led me to the work I am doing today.

I have been in therapy on and off for decades, and it is always amazing to me when I start with a therapist that by the end of our first session they all come back to the trauma with my uncle and say I have more work to do there. I am very grateful for the persistence of my therapists and their genius in knowing that trauma such as this takes many years of healing because there is layer upon layer that needs to be unearthed in order to finally release the true pain.

Healing our deep wounds is like peeling back the layers of an onion. The wound gets smaller and smaller, but until we can get to the core of the pain, there will still be an emotional charge around what happened. And the scary thing is this charge shows up in unexpected, irrational ways in our daily lives (such as yelling at my daughter for no reason, feeling less than at a luncheon where I am the guest speaker, or feeling loneliness in the midst of the happiest day of my life). Every time I talked about my uncle with a therapist, I got the feelings out and peeled back another layer. And then, I finally got to the core.

This was a truly powerful aha moment. Everything shifted for me. It was like an earthquake opened up the ground and swallowed that last piece of my shame, blame, and self-loathing. I could feel forever changed, from the inside out, in that moment. Remember, I grew up in a home where for as long as I could remember I was either taking care of my younger siblings or working; I did not have a "child's life" and had never, ever seen myself as a kid. I always felt like a grown-up who could take care of herself and knew better than to make the choices she made, so to think back and imagine me as a minor, a fourteen-year-old girl, like my daughter, blew me away inside, literally.

Forgiveness is not a gift for another person. At its core, it has nothing to do with anyone but you. Forgiveness is something that you do for yourself, so that the past no longer has a hold on you. But you do not have to reach a place of complete forgiveness to experience the benefits. They happen along each step of the way. As my daughter, Michelle Maros, says, "Forgiveness does not mean what happened was okay. It means not letting what happened take any more of your happiness."

One tool I used to heal was mantra writing. For each mantra-writing session, I'd write my concern or issue at the top of the page. In this case, I'd just write the word "uncle." I'd set the intention to forgive and release all the energy that kept me tied to what had happened. I would write my mantra, "My God and My All," over and over, focusing my full attention on it. Every time my mind started to wander, I'd bring it back to my mantra and my intention to heal from the trauma with my uncle.

When I first started this practice, I'd get emotional and think he didn't deserve my forgiveness. I wondered if

I really needed to do it. **But then I began to understand that this process was not about forgiving him—it was about forgiving myself.** Sometimes memories and difficult emotions would come up. Some days I could write only a couple of lines, and other days I filled four or five pages. Part of the healing for me was the consistency in every day returning to my intention to forgive and move forward. Mantra writing helped me sit with the emotions and not run. Little by little, I felt a release.

Today I feel free from what happened to me. When the topic of sexual abuse comes up, I no longer feel triggered. The final piece in my healing journey was being able to forgive myself. I was able to release the idea that there was something wrong with me.

I heal through meditation.

I heal through therapy.

I heal through writing.

I heal through teaching.

Barb Schmidt *is an author, a meditation teacher, and an activist.*

GO WHERE IT FEELS GOOD

A few years ago, I started walking every single day. Making and keeping this promise to myself was a testament to the growth I'd done over the years. At the time, everything felt demanding and heavy in my life, and I couldn't figure out how to offer myself any sort of relief. Life was full, work was busy, and I struggled to be and stay present. Reading *Do Walk*, a book about starting a regular walking practice, flipped a switch in me. To say it was transformative would be an understatement. I had no idea it would alter my relationship with my body, my mind, and my healing. Starting a walking practice was the last thing on my radar that I would think could monumentally shift the way I show up for myself—but needless to say, I am forever changed and have since tapped into my healing on an even deeper level. On my walks, I've cried, I've laughed to myself, and I've found peace. Emotionally, things have come up during each step that I don't think I could've processed sitting still. Reconnecting with myself each day was the gift I needed.

Walking clears my mind and opens me up to new avenues and roads back home to myself. The silence is liberating, the nature is fascinating, and the weather brings up different emotions every day. Even on my worst days, I walk. The consistency helps redirect my energy and reminds me to welcome gratitude into my space. It also reminds me to keep going. When I'm mid-walk and want to be home already, there's no quick way back—even if I decided to rush or run, there's no easy way around having to get myself back home. Each walk reminds me to keep putting one foot in front of the other. I look at healing through a similar lens. Coming back home to myself is a step-by-step process. Speeding through it won't bring me any closer to myself because I'll be missing things along the way.

Walking through my thoughts has become my go-to practice. Before I write, I walk. When I'm outside, I'm homing in on the smallest details in nature. I look up more. I pay close attention to how I'm feeling, moving, and being at that very moment. Coming back to the page after that feels full of new insight and grace for every place I've been, not just that morning's walk.

Facing my pain points and tenderness while I move and breathe with intention reminds me that there is healing in the simple things. We don't always have to be on a cushion meditating or on our knees praying to find the answers we are looking for. There will be moments where we must slowly and compassionately put one foot in front of the other, with no destination in sight. The author of *Do Walk*, Libby DeLana, who has since become a friend, writes, "Go gently, slow down, look up, and humbly learn." Her words often come to mind as I walk further into my healing and closer to myself. When I can't process my thoughts on paper, I walk, and I encourage my mind to go where it feels good. When we welcome a sense of ease in our lives, it takes the pressure off trying to solve our problems right away. Walking invites my whole self to be entirely present—tending to my feelings, thoughts, and emotions with more softness and consideration. It also reminds me that I am safe with myself and can trust the path I am on.

Healing our hearts takes a lot out of us. Emotionally, we can feel all over the place before we find our footing. My nudge to you, as you move through your healing, is to create a practice in your life that brings you peace. Let it extend a sense of connection to your story—past, present, and future. You don't always have to be in a place of profound processing. Welcome the slow and restful moments of healing that don't require heavy lifting. Maybe you want to start an intentional walking practice too, or perhaps your peace comes from painting, cooking, gardening, or jujitsu. No matter your path, offer yourself the space and time to show up fully without your to-do list. Make a space for yourself that is all about feeling good.

We cannot run from the things that scare us forever. Rushing our process because we want it to be over already doesn't serve us. We can try to bypass the hard work, but what good will that do, really? We can't suppress our pain and expect to not come crumbling down one day. Rather, finding what feels good and safe on this healing journey is critical to making progress. If you can't write because it feels like your voice is caught in your throat, do something else that offers you a sense of belonging, refuge, and comfort. Make your healing practice your own. You don't always have to be unpacking the depths of your soul on the page. Sometimes you just need a soft place to land that restores your mind and body and reassures you that you can get through it.

We can feel stuck in our efforts to heal and face the difficult things that emerge. This next practice offers you a way to get unstuck when the path feels precarious.

Notes to Self

Healing our hearts requires us to be kinder to ourselves. Each week for the next month, I invite you to write a kind note to your self. Pick one day a week—I like to write my letters on Sundays—and set some intentional time to meet yourself exactly where you are.

Perhaps you walked through a challenging week, and you want to use the adversity you faced as an opportunity to reflect on how you can support yourself in the days ahead. Or maybe you had a fantastic week, and you let yourself feel and celebrate all that came up. Use these letters as an opportunity to guide yourself closer to yourself.

Following are some freewriting prompts. Don't edit yourself. Just flow.

Dear Self, thank you for being . . .

Dear Self, I am proud of you for . . .

Dear Self, I know things feel . . .

Dear Self, you are deserving of . . .

Journaling

Layers to Healing
Tabitha Brown

Alex Elle: Who are you and what do you do?

Tabitha Brown: I am Tabitha Brown. I am a wife, woman, mother, and believer. I spread love by being myself and being free. Some people would say that I am an entertainer. I'm also an actress and a foodie.

AE: How has healing shown up in your life? And was there something in particular that shaped you to do the most healing?

TB: I think healing is a journey. It's not a permanent destination. It's continuous. Healing started for me in 2016 when I got sick. I was not well inside. Something was attacking my body; it was an autoimmune condition. Doctors couldn't diagnose or figure out what was going on with me. During that time, it felt like my mind was also under attack. Depression and anxiety were very bad for me. In 2017, after having what I call my final call with Jesus in my bathroom, I said: "God, if you heal me, you can have me. I won't try to live my life my way anymore. I will live it the way you created me to be."

I really meant it that day. And each day since then, it's been like taking layers off. I feel that part of my sickness in my body happened because I wasn't being my authentic self, so I couldn't breathe. The true me couldn't breathe. She was suffocating.

The moment I started taking off those layers and making a choice to heal and be free, my whole life began to change. And I've been doing that ever since. The best thing I ever gave myself was the freedom to be. That in itself is healing. I'll never stop healing. I'll be healing until the day I leave here. It's my obligation to remain in a healing space.

AE: You mentioned peeling back layers. What layer are you in now?

TB: I'm in the layer of understanding. When you're going through things, you don't understand why, but once you get through it and you reach a new place in your life, you find peace and have insight when you look back. Often we realize that certain things had to happen to teach us something. I'm at that level of understanding because people look at my life and say, "You're living your dreams, and all these amazing things are happening."

Amazing things are happening, and I'm very grateful. But I can clearly see now why God had me go through these different phases of life. I didn't always understand the path I was on. I know now that what I walked through led me to this part of the understanding. I get excited about my life layers now because new lessons emerge as I pull them back.

AE: What event during the pandemic prompted you to dive deeper into your healing?

TB: During the pandemic is when I first got on TikTok. I didn't want to get on there because it's a young-people app, but my daughter convinced me. I ended up getting on the app and started doing my cooking videos. One day I did an inspirational video that resonated with people. I looked at the comments, and the outpouring of love was amazing. Folks were saying things like "That message was for me" and "Your voice sounds like a warm hug." All those comments made me realize that when we encourage others, we also encourage ourselves. Doing inspirational videos helped me help myself.

I took on the responsibility of making these videos that I felt were necessary for the world. In a time when everything felt very scary, I chose to show up for others while showing up for myself, and I did that every day. I did a video whether or not I was cooking or inspiring, making people laugh or making them cry. Making videos was so rewarding because it taught me patience. It taught me how to be still. It taught me how to listen even more. And it taught me how to heal others through myself.

There is beauty and power in making people feel better. I wasn't doing work I was proud of at one point in my career. I was doing work because I needed a check. But doing those videos made me proud, and they healed the part of me that I used to be kind of ashamed of for some

of the work that I did in the past that didn't mean anything. I had to get to a place of understanding, which
is the layer I'm in now. If I had never done things that
I wasn't necessarily proud of, I wouldn't understand the
feeling of wholeness that I feel now for doing something
good that's healing. That's what I discovered, and it made
me better as a woman, as a wife, as a mother. I feel more
rooted in my purpose now.

AE: What creative modalities do you use to heal?

TB: I talk to my mom like she's here. Before my mom
passed, she told me that she would be wherever I call her
to be. She said, "Whenever you need to release something or speak to me or feel me, you can just begin to
speak and know that I'm there with you." So when things
are going well, I talk to my mom. And when they're going
not so well, I still talk to her, no matter where I am. I find
comfort in that conversation we had and remember that
she's always there, wherever I call her to be. That helps
me heal in moments when I need it. Talking to my mom
and calling on her spirit is a continuous tool I use to
navigate healing and grief. It's my way of celebrating her
existence and acknowledging that she's still with me.

AE: Has your relationship with God and faith changed
since the passing of your mother, and, if so, in what ways?

TB: My faith got stronger when my mother died. She
had ALS [amyotrophic lateral sclerosis, also known as
Lou Gehrig's disease] and we knew she was going to die.
At the very end of her life, she was, essentially, trapped
inside of her body. She could not move anything but her

lips and eyes. She passed on a Sunday. The Friday before, I spent the night at the hospital. When I woke up that Friday morning, she motioned with her lips to tell me she was going home on Sunday. I thought the doctor came in and told her she was being discharged while I was sleeping. I asked her, "The doctor said you're going home on Sunday?" I was reading her lips carefully, and she said no. She looked up to the sky, as if to say, "I'm going home, to heaven, on Sunday."

My mom was on life support, and I had power of attorney, so I asked her, "Mama, are you sure you want to come off the machine?" And she said, "Yes, God said it's time."

My mom instructed me to call all of her family and friends to see her before she went home. When the doctor came in, I gave him the news. He told me that no one should be in the room because her last moments of life would be disturbing, and she'd start having convulsions. My mother said no to that. She wanted everyone in the room with her. She refuted what the doctor said would happen.

When Sunday came, the machines and lights were turned off. Thirty of us gathered in the room singing songs and celebrating her life. It was so peaceful the entire time, so much so that we didn't even know she had passed. She never gasped for a last breath. She never shook. She didn't do anything. She just smiled. The doctors were dumbfounded. This experience made me a stronger believer in my faith and God. I am so connected to the other side.

AE: How does emotional rest refuel your healing?

TB: When you know yourself and what you want, and what you can handle and can't, you can take a minute to pause and reflect. I'm very connected with myself, and I put myself first all the time. I know when things aren't good for me and when they're disrupting my spirit, and then I give myself the space to rest and heal. When things linger or bother me, I don't ignore them or act like they don't exist. I talk about them and address them so that I don't let them live inside me—because everything isn't mine to carry. Emotional rest is learning to look at what is yours and what is not. When we hold on to things that don't belong to us, it can disrupt our rest, physically and emotionally. Being completely connected and open with myself about who I am brings me the inner peace, emotional rest, and clarity I need in life.

AE: How do you heal?

TB: I heal by staying true to myself.

Tabitha Brown *is an actress, an author, and a social media personality.*

GROWING IN GRATITUDE

At the tail end of 2020, I had an anxiety attack—one that led me down the road of insomnia, hair pulling, and utter inner chaos. I felt completely lost, with nowhere to go. I hadn't been that depressed, burned out, and emotionally overwhelmed in years. Even when we feel like things can't get any worse, things can. The only thing I could remember to do was find gratitude in making it to another day—and even that felt hard to do. I know this may sound cliché, but when you feel like you have nothing left, you still have your breath. Holding on to that perspective gave me the slightest glimmer of hope.

Healing during this time took on a whole new shape. I'd been at rock bottom before—only this time I was married with three kids, a thriving career, and so much more on my plate to handle and take care of. Trying to heal felt absurd. There were too many other things to do first. So I decided to start small. Starting a daily gratitude list was my first baby step into chipping away at my pain. Talking to my doctor about medication options was the second. I could not keep quieting my pain with the hope of "I'll be fine tomorrow." It'd been months, and tomorrow never came. Something had to change.

At first, I was annoyed at myself for having to start over. I kept hearing my inner critic's voice in my head:

If you had just taken care of yourself from the beginning, you wouldn't be here.

You love to push yourself past your limits, don't you?

Why can't you learn from your past mistakes? What's wrong with you?

Quieting that negative inner chatter took a lot of patience. There were days when I wanted to give up, stay in bed, and vanish into thin air. Getting up was a struggle. Being present was damn near impossible. Having a beginner's mind didn't feel like a blessing—in fact, it felt like the complete opposite. But if healing has taught me anything, it's that I must stay open to learning.

Practicing gratitude changed my life for the better. With the help of my medication and my journal, I started to see the light in the small things, like having enough energy to get out of bed or to eat a nourishing meal. Some days, those were milestones for me. My depression and anxiety had gotten me so down that I was floating through my days. I was so far removed from my life that I couldn't remember waking up or going to sleep.

During this time, I found a book called *Wake Up Grateful* by Kristi Nelson. It would further help me unfold into a more healed and present version of myself. There's a line in that book that I will never forget: "Gratitude is great, but gratefulness is greater. . . . Gratefulness is a *way of being* that helps us focus our attention and navigate our lives with gratitude as our compass." Reframing what I thought it meant to be grateful and express gratitude completely rearranged my thoughts. I'd been doing it all wrong. I wasn't focused. I wasn't present. And because of that, I wasn't able to see my path or trust the detours. When we express gratitude for what we have, even in our waves of anxiety and sadness, we learn how to cope a little better. We learn how to hang in there a little longer.

That passage opened my eyes to the possibility of being present while also being in pain. It reminded me of the duality that life offers us daily. When it comes to healing, there is no black or white. A lot of our healing takes place in the middle. I tell my students and clients to get comfortable with being in the middle of healing—there is something to learn there too. We don't always have to be unraveling to experience our healing. We don't always need to get over that big hurdle to experience wholeness. There will be moments when we must sit with being in the middle and be okay with having nothing more to do than be there, be still, and be grateful.

Feeling engulfed by darkness was a clear invitation to actively look at and be present with myself. So many things needed my attention, like my constant dishonoring of my personal boundaries. There were days when I'd write down, *I'm grateful for not abandoning myself today* or *I am grateful for honoring my boundaries*. It was those short passages that reeled me in and asked me to look closer at what landed me back into my dark place. My gratitude practice wasn't a fluffy or forced thing—it was my lifeline and the encouragement I needed to look my inner turmoil in the face and say *I see you*.

Alice Walker once said, "'Thank you' is the best prayer that anyone could say. . . . [It] expresses extreme gratitude, humility, understanding." I wanted to embody that within myself. Often we express thanks to others, but rarely do we hold an attitude of appreciation toward ourselves. I'd been doing so much without paying an ounce of attention to myself, let alone offering the gift of gratitude to myself. It's almost like I ignored myself to stay connected and committed to everyone else. There was no balance between prioritizing myself and showing up for those around me. I was living proof that being all in on one thing while sacrificing yourself serves no one at the end of the day. Gratitude practice showed me how to zoom in on my life and pay close attention to the small moments of joy, not just the large ones. If we don't pay closer attention, we will miss what's right in front of us.

Gratitude is now the center of my self-care practice. It holds me accountable and keeps me present. It welcomes me to get curious and reminds me not to take my one life for granted. Moving through this dark season of life, I reminded myself that when I am grieving or in pain, I'm still worthy and grateful. It might sound counterintuitive to be grateful for our struggles, but without them we wouldn't know resilience. To know joy is to know pain, and as Buddhism teaches, to live is to suffer. Gratitude is the nudge to remember our aliveness so that we can know joy and also recognize it when it shows up. When we aren't in tune with ourselves, we aren't alive enough to feel, see, and hear it all—the good and the painful.

Gratitude isn't about taking inventory of the good things. It's about making space in your heart, mind, and body to experience the mundane. Living fully and intentionally is an invitation to prioritize your own life, to ensure that you are giving yourself the time and space to become who you want to be. We miss things when our heads are down. We can't see hope if we refuse to unlatch from what we think we know about the pain we're clinging to. Yes, feel all of your feelings, and also let yourself rest from trying to figure out how not to be hurting. The low points you face won't be your last. The gratification of making it through will greet you over and over again. Don't discredit how far you've come when you're in the middle of it all.

Thirty Days of Gratitude

Start a gratitude list in your journal or on your phone, and each morning and night, jot down one thing you're grateful for. Invite a friend to do this with you over the next thirty days. Send a text or have a short phone call about what you felt grateful for each day. Take note of how you feel at the start of day one and at the end of the thirty days. Have a conversation about how hard or easy it was for you to keep up with the practice. Observe what words or things came up multiple times. Talk through why. This exercise invites you and the ones you love to pay close attention to not only your mood, but also your life. Healing our hearts is slow and steady work; celebrate the ways you've evolved by committing to this practice.

Conversation

Gratitude for What's Hard

In this practice, we'll be practicing gratitude for the hard things that offer us opportunities to dive deeper into our healing. Find a comfortable place to sit or lie. Bring to mind an instance that challenged you. Perhaps you had a hard conversation with a loved one, or you needed to advocate for yourself at work. Or maybe, like me, you experienced a difficult time with your mental health. Allow yourself to intentionally think about it and greet whatever comes to mind with a sense of gratitude. If it feels difficult to do this, close your eyes and take a deep breath. That alone is a way to express gratitude to yourself.

(Inhale.)

I am grateful that I am able to hold space and breathe through this hard thing.

(Exhale.)

Meditation

Healing in Travel
Sara Kuburic

Alex Elle: Who are you and what do you do?

Sara Kuburic: I don't know why this is a tricky question. Tying to summarize who I am is difficult. When I reflect on who I am, what speaks to who I am the most is that I live as a nomad. I'm passionate about advocating for mental health, and I love supporting other women to reach their goals. Professionally, I'm an existential therapist, consultant, and writer.

AE: How has healing shown up in your life? And was there something in particular that shaped you?

SK: Healing happened accidentally, at first. I didn't realize how wounded I was until I began to heal. My healing started to emerge as I traveled. There are so many clichés about nomads, and I recognize the incredible privilege of living like this. When I initially started to travel, I had $800 and no idea where I was going or what I was doing. All I knew was that the version of myself that I was experiencing was not me and that the pain I was experiencing

I couldn't face or handle if I stayed in the same circumstance. And so, at twenty years old, I decided to travel. The most surprising part of it is how much it did heal me. Looking back, I think it started as escapism, and then it became a very intentional thing that nourished me into the version of myself that I am today.

AE: What has living as a nomad taught you about change and your ability to heal in different places?

SK: It was difficult for me at first. I didn't enjoy it because it was so much change, and I felt unanchored. What ended up happening was that this life forced me to anchor within myself because it was the only consistent thing I had. That was powerful for me because I couldn't use my routine, context, or support system. Initially, I didn't have a support system directly with me when I was traveling. And so it forced me to focus on my relationship with myself in a way that, at the time, was quite uncomfortable. It also triggered me in unique ways. I'm from the Balkans, so being a white female and experiencing different cultures opened my eyes. For example, my experience is very different when I'm in France versus in Jordan. This was important to see because it got me to stop, look at myself, and be aware of my privilege. Different cultures also came with varying views of the world, from religions to diverse perspectives on mental health and healing. And experiencing all of this encouraged me not to be so narrow-minded. When I was in my early twenties, I used to think I knew everything. Like most people that age, you assume you know things more than you actually do. Traveling was a beautiful and necessary way to realize how little I knew. There was a massive element of deconstruction that helped me heal. I needed to deconstruct myself to have enough space to construct who I wanted to become.

AE: What creative modalities have you used to heal?

SK: Mainly writing, now. But when I was younger, I used to dance and write poetry. Dancing helped me feel embodied, grounded, and expressive. I come from a culture where expressing pain wasn't something acceptable. I was surrounded by people who forced gratitude. Dance allowed me to feel things and express things in a way that I couldn't verbally do. I started to write poetry when I was ten. It gave me a place to process what was happening. I always wanted words to be beautiful, even if the meaning was painful. I always found beauty in pain as well. I think a bit of that stems from surviving wars and being an immigrant, and just being surrounded by a lot of pain as a child but still finding beauty around me. As I grew up, I found a deeper connection to my voice in writing.

AE: How do you heal?

SK: I heal by feeling. I heal by writing. I heal by experiencing. I heal by connecting.

Sara Kuburic *is a therapist who specializes in identity, relationships, and moral trauma.*

REDISCOVERING AND BEING IN JOY

Something that you may discover during your healing practice is that some of your loved ones will not be able to understand your process. If healing has taught me anything, it's that not everyone can walk with us as we move through our process of self-discovery. A big part of people's assumptions is that just because you're healing, you must be sad, hurting, or suffering through it. That isn't always the case. And it certainly doesn't ring true forever.

Healing isn't linear. It's fluid, choppy, messy, and complicated. It's liberating, expansive, transformative, and intuitive. As you move through healing your heart, you can and will experience joy. There may be some cloudy days. Healing our hearts begs us to open ourselves up so that we can delight in all that's in store for us.

Experiencing pleasure as you heal is possible. I never thought my neighbor would smile or speak to me, but she did. There were times when I would cry for days because of how broken I felt. Those days eventually passed, even when they seemed like they wouldn't. Everything has its season and its lesson.

Being with our wounds—fully grieving without rushing and judgment, and unraveling our trauma—is just as important as healing them. Feeling like we don't know joy is just as important as learning how to see and accept it when it shows up. That is how we stay curious and open while healing. We do not have to drown in misery because we're healing our hearts.

Relief and opportunity can be found in the depths of our soul work. Giving ourselves permission to put down the heaviness and hold lightness is our birthright. Life and the things we go through do not always have to be a struggle. There's a lot of emphasis on the inner work we do—heal, mend, and move through it. But something that isn't encouraged, talked about, or celebrated enough is stepping away from the healing to just let yourself be as you are.

I invite you to pause as many times as you need to during the course of this work, especially if you're feeling over-whelmed or stuck. I even encourage you to take a break from it all. Emotional rest is a breath of fresh air, and you deserve to not constantly be in "fixer" mode. The goal is not to overthink or force healing to happen or joy to emerge. It will naturally take its course. Instead, make space on the page to see where it's showing up in your life or where you want it to emerge. The step after that is being open to welcoming the glory that makes it to you without questioning whether you deserve it.

When I think about healing my heart, I think about the freedom to live and love with no restraints. I know firsthand how terrifying it feels to not harden your heart after walking through darkness and pain. However, this is a challenge to face your fears around giving and receiv-ing love. Welcoming and experiencing joy is something that must be practiced. It may not always feel easy to acknowledge or accept, but keep the door open for its arrival. Give yourself permission.

Here are some phrases to keep close as you heal your heart and make space for joy:

I give myself permission to speak up.

I give myself permission to not know what's next.

I give myself permission to change my mind.

I give myself permission to heal without judgment.

I give myself permission to release self-doubt.

I give myself permission to try new things.

I give myself permission to be alone and be okay.

I give myself permission to have boundaries.

I give myself permission to not have it all planned out.

I give myself permission to fail and get back up.

I give myself permission to be a vessel for joy.

WRITING LETTERS TO JOY

When we are in the trenches of our pain, it can be unimaginable to think we will make it through to the other side. Sifting through the childhood trauma that had resurfaced was one of my biggest challenges. I remember saying to my therapist, "I worked so hard to heal and now I am back to being broken." I desperately wanted my joy back. It was exhausting revisiting the things I couldn't change, even though I knew it was necessary. She encouraged me to do some inner-child work in my journal.

"How would you have protected your younger self?" she asked.

I had just stopped crying, and my puffy face and red eyes looked back at me through the telehealth screen. Regret for signing myself up for therapy started to flood my mind. "I don't know," I said with a heavy heart.

"You've come so far, Alex," she said with compassion in her voice. "I know this is hard work—and I also know that you know the answer to that question, even if it feels far away."

She was right. I did have the answers, and even if it felt tough to peel back the layers and look at everything underneath, I had to give it a shot. Starting with joy felt easier for me. For so long I thought that joy didn't belong to me or was out of my reach. Choosing to center joy as I was working through my healing gave me some hope that things could get better. What I realized in therapy was that I wasn't looking for my pain or trauma to be solved. I knew that wasn't constructive. What I wanted from the work I was doing was to uncover the possibilities that addressing my healing head-on could offer. I knew that joy could find me, because I'd seen and felt glimpses of it before. Learning to balance the healing with the expectation of joy emerging after we think it has evaded us is a gift that only we can give to ourselves. Rather than wait for it to find me, I decided to be proactive and invite joy back into my life.

My first letter to joy started like this:

Dear Joy,

I am looking forward to seeing you again. Sometimes it feels like you're avoiding me, but in the end you always return. Thank you for giving me the space I need to heal and process life without you. If I didn't know pain, I wouldn't know you. And while I can't say I've enjoyed walking through my life's struggles without you close by or in tow, I am learning how to love myself when you're away and not just when you're here.

Reading this note out loud took some time, but I recorded myself reading it and played it back multiple times. This served as a reminder to create a safe space for myself internally. I encourage you to write your own letter to joy following my example above. This is a helpful practice because it allows you to make space and room in your life for something other than your struggles. You are not your pain. Give yourself permission to welcome, acknowledge, and feel joy.

Receiving Joy

For this meditation practice, I invite you to get comfortable and focus on your breath. Read the following script silently or out loud, or record it on your phone and listen to it when you need a positive reminder. Take a deep breath in and exhale through an open mouth before reading.

I am finding moments of joy by not rushing my process.

I don't have to see the light at the end of the tunnel today, but I am open to receiving joy when it arrives.

I am finding moments of joy by paying closer attention to my wants and needs.

I don't have to shrink myself or silence my voice as I heal.

I am finding moments of joy by addressing my healing head-on.

I don't have to hide from my pain anymore.

I am finding moments of joy by holding space for both my healing and my pain.

I don't have to pick one or the other. They can both exist and teach me something.

Meditation

Celebrate Joy

Recalling moments of joy can lift our spirits and break cycles of despair. But it takes practice to focus on what is good and beautiful in our past. Sometimes our difficult memories demand the bulk of our attention.

In your journal, write about three joyful memories. These could be a small moment of pleasure, a happy experience with loved ones, or something that made you laugh until you cried. As you write, sink into the memory. Where were you? What did the experience feel like in your body? How can you recapture some of that joy today?

Return to this practice when you feel overwhelmed by difficult memories. Lean into the good. Fill yourself up with all the joy. Feel the pleasure in your bones.

Journaling

Healing:
An Active Process
Dr. Yaba Blay

Alex Elle: Who are you and what do you do?

Dr. Yaba Blay: You're asking me this question in the midst of what feels like a prolonged identity crisis, and maybe it's not a crisis—perhaps it's healing. I'm an educator. I'm a storyteller. I'm a creative. I used to call myself the "Queen of Bright Ideas" because I love ideating. I believe I'm a healer. I say that hesitantly, only because I know that people have their own notions of who a healer is or what healing is. Part of my healing is seeing myself in the mirror. I'm actively working to name myself and acknowledge what I do and who I feel I am.

I have my PhD in African American studies and women and gender studies. When I was a graduate student, one of the only career paths ever discussed was a tenure-track position. Being in academics has led me to realize its impact on me. We are valued based on teaching, research, and service. When I graduated, I didn't have a job. Unlike many of my colleagues, I didn't have a

tenure-track position because I chose to write my disser-
tation and not go on the job market. I graduated—I was
done, but I didn't have a job. It felt like I went on a journey of position after position, whether it was a combina-
tion of administration and faculty or teaching faculty. I've
always taught, but I still didn't have that tenure position.
At the time, initially, it felt like a failure. I can see the
blessing in it now because it afforded me a particular
level of freedom. I've always done creative work, or what
felt like my own independent research, "on the side,"
while also teaching—not for the purpose of getting aca-
demic credit for it, but doing the work because I *wanted*
to do the work. I am so very much connected to my work.
It reflects my life, my curiosities, and my journey. That's
one of the greatest gifts I got being trained in Black studies at Temple University, home of Afrocentricity.

AE: What did you learn about yourself and healing while
teaching, studying, and being at Temple University?

YB: I was very much grounded in African-centeredness as
part of my research methodology. I was allowed to center
myself. We didn't take on the traditional path of objectiv-
ity where you have to somehow distance yourself from
the work. In contrast, we had to be connected to the work
in the same way we had to be connected to our people.
And so it's always been a gift because all of my work starts
with me. I don't have to apologize for what I'm interested
in doing. My work on colorism is because I grew up with
dark skin and kinky hair as a first-generation Ghanaian in
New Orleans. I've always been very aware of what I look

193

like and what that means in terms of how people see and estimate my value. Colorism is my life. Doing work to address colorism is part of my healing. Before starting my PhD, I had a master's in counseling psychology. I was a licensed and practicing therapist. I was drawn to the cognitive behavioral approach primarily because of the connection between what we think and what we do.

In 2019, I left the academy—it didn't feel like a permanent departure and still doesn't, but I decided not to be on that wheel for now. I wasn't happy. The work that sustained and fulfilled me was the work I was doing "on the side." I love teaching, but having to function within the confines of the academy was a lot. I didn't know what I was going to do, and still, I left my position in North Carolina, moved back to Philadelphia, where my daughter and granddaughters are, and went on unemployment. Then COVID hit, and thankfully, my social media community honestly sustained me with love offerings and such. And I hustled—I consulted, I did speaking engagements—but I didn't have the "stability" of the direct deposit. But there was a sense of freedom in that for me.

AE: Was there something in particular that shaped you to do the most healing?

YB: I don't see healing as an end point. It's an ongoing and lifelong process. I also don't see healing as a thing that is just like a blanket over us. There are parts of us that need healing in different ways. And so I know that there are parts of me that have healed. There are parts of me that have begun to heal. There are parts of me that may never heal. When I self-reflect and look at my identity and sense of self, healing has shown up through education and by actively learning how to do my own soul work. However, I realize there are parts of me that still need healing. The little Yaba still needs to make sense of certain things that she's experienced; a grown Yaba is trying to make sense of what she's encountering today. There's healing that comes when I see Black folks thriving and surviving and resisting. I can be moved to tears by historical photos and stories. To think of who our people have always been—it's like an act of connectedness that is proof that our history doesn't just live way back when. Healing is an active process; to be in it is healing.

AE: What creative modalities have you used or are you using to heal yourself?

YB: Music and dancing bring me joy—and so does playing on the internet. Things that bring me joy help me heal. What's so interesting to me is that (and this could be my Gemini rising) I love the idea of there being a Dr. Blay and a Yaba. There's the work, but then there's also the person. And so whatever you think a scholar or professor or a public person is, I can be that. But I'm also going to always be Yaba. I'm silly. I love to laugh. I love social media—Instagram and TikTok in partic- ular. I curate weekly videos from these platforms for my online community, and it's so healing to gather the material and see that we find joy actively, even in the face of white supremacy. I don't know if anybody else can do it like us. Our people know how to have a good time. Instinctually, whether we can name it or not, we know that physically in our bodies, there are endorphins and other things signaled when we laugh and smile. That is healing for me.

Dr. Yaba Blay *is a professor, scholar-activist, public speaker, cultural worker, and consultant.*

RELEASING WHAT NO LONGER SERVES YOU

Throughout these steps, we've been slowly learning to identify the stories, self-doubt, and pain that no longer serve us. It is time to let those things go. If you don't allow yourself to let go, you will find it painfully difficult to heal. I know it may feel overwhelming or easier said than done to release our past trauma as our truth, to let go of those feelings of shame, guilt, and self-doubt. To part ways from what is weighing us down takes courage and the willingness to be vulnerable with yourself and others.

Growing up, some of us may not have been given the space to practice naming what we needed or wanted. As we look at what it means to release in order to receive, the invitation is to do your best to leave the learned behavior of not naming your needs and vocalizing your wants at the door. When we release what is no longer serving us or what is hindering us from truly peeling back the layers of healing, we make space for new ways to explore who we are, the life we want to create, and the relationships we want to have with ourselves and others.

Letting go makes room for something greater, even when it's hard. We have the power to unfurl and bloom. Abundance is waiting. We always have a choice in our healing. Commit to no longer waiting for something magical or devastating to happen before you start doing your soul work. Choosing to begin exactly where you are in life is liberating and gracious. We are never too broken to start. Even when we feel like we're in pieces, we can release the belief that brokenness is where we find our wholeness.

Letting go is a choice that we all must make.

We can stay stuck in the cycles that are holding us back, or we can shed the things that are no longer serving us. Releasing what is no longer serving you will finally allow you to start filling your space and life with the things that truly nurture your soul.

Connect to your power by tapping into self-trust and releasing self-doubt. Everything that you're carrying that you're scared to put down was passed on to you by others. You can choose to no longer cling to things that are not your narrative and your truth. Remember what you are capable of.

You are well on your way to healing your heart on a deeper level. Even if you think you've done this work already and you don't need to let go of anything else, think twice about that. Scan your life, your relationships, your patterns, and your habits and see what may be keeping you stuck, scared, or disconnected. Remember, we are forever students in this work and life. Stay committed to the different ways you may need to shift and adjust.

I invite you to write down everything you're letting go of in the next exercise. Look at it all and release it—no more excuses for holding on to things, people, or patterns that are keeping you emotionally hostage. A new beginning is on the horizon. Leave your insecurities and self-judgment at your feet. Part ways and make peace with the separation.

Releasing Jar

In this practice, you'll need a jar with a lid and small pieces of paper. Label your jar "I Am Letting Go." Have fun decorating your jar. You can use stickers, markers, glitter, ribbons, paint, or anything else that feels fun and exciting. Let your inner child play, make a mess, and let loose. This jar is going to be central to your healing practice over the next several weeks. For the next month, every day, you be will writing down something that you're letting go of.

Keep the jar somewhere you can see it. Whatever comes to mind, put it on a note, fold it up, and drop it in your jar. At the end of the month, it's time to celebrate yourself for all that you've let go. Maybe you cook yourself a nice meal and read through your notes. Maybe you light a fire in your backyard and make a ritual out of burning your notes. Maybe you do this with a friend and you get together to compare the things in your jars. Notice how it feels to release the bad so that you can make more space for the good. Letting go is hard work. It takes energy and patience. The repeated practice of naming the things that are no longer serving you and tucking them away in the jar will help your brain let go, too.

Journaling

Healing in the Answers
Lisa Olivera

I continuously return to myself in many ways, from my
work as a therapist to my relationships and even in my
healing process. I have had a tendency in the past to asso-
ciate who I am and what I do with my career. I've been
trying to move out of that and embrace the presence
I want to be in the world. I'm working on letting who I am
in the world today be enough. Right now, that includes
doing therapy and holding space. It also takes shape
through writing, sharing, creating, and connecting.

What initially led me to know that I needed healing is
dealing with abandonment and separation from my birth
mother and being an adoptee. I struggled with my identity and did not feel like I was enough. I constantly questioned why I was here and whether or not I belonged.

Those questions haunted me for a long time, and I was
silent about them for equally as long. I held a massive
weight by myself and was so afraid to be honest about
that. It eventually got to the point where I didn't want to

live anymore. Being faced with that reckoning, I realized that things could not continue how they were. And I wouldn't be able to live if things continued to stay the same. Something needed to shift.

Being suicidal forced me into the process of discovering that healing was even possible. It was a very slow process and one that I held a lot of shame about for a long time. I know now that everything I went through was purposeful and necessary. It gave me the life that I needed and didn't know I could have at the time. Having a healthy relationship with myself felt far away at one point. I realize now that healing is a continuous process.

There are moments in my life now where I circle back to some of those old stories, and it's proof that my healing is not done just because I've learned a lot of lessons and cultivated some wisdom along the way. I still have to do the work. Different seasons require different kinds of healing. Each season looks and feels different at various times. Certain life circumstances bring up old parts of me that I must remember to keep tending to. It's an ongoing journey that I know will never end, and it's a relief not to think that it's supposed to.

Going through therapy led me to understand the importance of finding answers to questions that I had. For years, I didn't let myself explore—until this point in my life. The catalyst for even deeper healing started when I decided to look for my birth family. This led me to finding my sister through Ancestry.com, which I never anticipated would happen. It opened up so much goodness and also so much grief. That experience allowed me to see parts of myself that I couldn't have possibly seen without having them reflected by these people I had this innate biological connection to, especially my sister. Connecting with her and meeting her for the first time several years ago validated the need to understand my identity, to know where I came from. It helped me unpack and explore the innate desire to be connected to people who are part of me. Meeting her was probably the first time that I truly felt like I wasn't alone in the world.

There were times where I had consciously said, *I'm not alone*. But connecting with my sister, I had an in-my-body sense of, *Wow, I'm really not alone*. That brought up so many feelings. I was grateful and grieving. There was a lot of grief for the amount of time I spent away from her and for the years that I spent yearning for a sense of belonging, not knowing that it was out there or that I would ever get to touch it. Since then, a big part of my healing has been unraveling, feeling alone while allowing myself to be connected. To feel seen in other spaces, which I had shut myself off from for a long time. Connecting with my sister showed me the areas I still needed to nurture in myself. I am still integrating and learning how to do that to this day. But meeting her, and eventually meeting my birth mother, allowed me to get some answers to the questions I had been asking my entire life. In a way, it gave me the courage to face myself.

Over the years, as I've explored my healing story, time in nature has been therapeutic and an avenue of creativity for me. Being in beautiful places and deep breathing allows me to tap into a part of myself that feels nourishing. Writing has also been vital in my process of healing. Over the years, it's shifted from writing from a place of pain. Instead, I began writing as a way of actually understanding myself. Asking reflective questions started to not feel as hard. Healing through writing allowed me to explore myself on a deeper level. I wasn't just processing everything that was wrong; I also began to discover self-awareness. I started to see who I was.

Emotional rest has been a must on this journey of connection, discovery, and finding my answers. Without it, healing can become a to-do list, ultimately defeating the purpose. It's really easy to forget that when we're bombarded with everyone else's healing journey and different modalities online. As a therapist, I've grown to know that I have to be intentional about resting, taking a step back, and living in my own life. It's hard work and requires intentional effort. Still, I am not supposed to be constantly healing and growing and working on myself; I don't need to turn myself into a project. The constant cycle of self-improvement doesn't nourish me.

As I look back on my life, I realize that I heal by slowing down enough to listen to myself, by being willing to ask what's there and then answering honestly. And by continuously trying to meet myself where I am—moment to moment—and letting that be enough, over and over again, forever.

Lisa Olivera *is a writer and therapist.*

Dear Reader,

You are now at the end of *How We Heal*. Thank you for sharing space with me. I hope the work and stories in this collection left you feeling seen, safe, supported, and less alone.

Allow grace to meet you exactly where you are. My wish is that these pages offered you tools to support you in your journey, whether you're just starting out or deep in this work. I hope you return to the passages that resonated the most over and over again. You are so deserving of healing, changing, and growing. I know that this work can feel heavy and hard to sift through, but take your time. Your healing isn't going anywhere. You don't have to figure it out today or tomorrow. Just be willing to try your best whenever you're ready.

Let yourself be a work in progress. There is a lot to unpack and sort through. Rushing through it will not make the healing less challenging or more complete. You do not have to hide from yourself any longer. You can show up and start your healing with a pen and paper. I know how intimidating that can feel. I know how hard it can be to allow vulnerability to lead the way, but shame and guilt are not safe spaces for you to linger in. Part ways with them and remember the life and healing you say you want to have. You can do hard things and create the life you desire even if those around you don't get it or aren't ready to understand your path.

We heal day by day, moment by moment, page by page. Stay soft with yourself, friends. I am rooting for you and cheering you on from afar. Make space for falling apart, failing, and trying again. You can and will heal—slowly but surely.

Big love,
Alex Elle

To my husband, I love you beyond words and am so grateful for your unwavering support and pep talks. You are my soft place to land. Thank you for being my mirror when my vision isn't clear.

To my children, I see you and adore you. You are the reason I heal with intention.

To Denisio and Racheal, thank you for taking my random phone calls and listening to the good and not-so-good renditions of this book. I needed your love, support, and nudges to go deeper. Your attention and patience mean more than you know.

To my mother and grandmother, you helped pave the way. Without you there would be no me. It's been beautiful getting to know you both as women. Your stories have shown me so much about grace, compassion, and connection. You both continue to help me heal along the way.

To my agent, Cindy Uh. You are a dream in human form. How did I get so lucky? I could not do this work without you. Thank you for being such a rock and place of peace throughout this process. You're a real one.

To my editors, Rachel Hiles, Sarah Billingsley, and Leigh Saffold, and designer, Vanessa Dina, your kindness, grace, and advocacy will be held close forever. Thank you for seeing and believing in my dream.

To the entire Chronicle Books team, your belief in my work is so important to me. Thank you for all your hard work and effort. I am proud to publish books with such a thoughtful and kind house.

To Dr. Yaba Blay, Tabitha Brown, Dr. Thema Bryant, Glennon Doyle, Luvvie Ajayi Jones, Nneka Julia, Sara Kuburic, Chriselle Lim, Morgan Harper Nichols, Lisa Olivera, Megan Rapinoe, Barb Schmidt, and Nedra Glover Tawwab, your stories will stick with me forever. Thank you for your vulnerability, sisterhood, and honesty. Our conversations have forever changed me.

To every reader of my books, students of my courses, and my community on- and offline, this collection wouldn't have been possible without your unwavering love and support. Thank you for trusting me and being on this journey with me.

Chronicle Books publishes distinctive books and gifts. From award-winning children's titles, bestselling cookbooks, and eclectic pop culture to acclaimed works of art and design, stationery, and journals, we craft publishing that's instantly recognizable for its spirit and creativity. Enjoy our publishing and become part of our community at www.chroniclebooks.com.